Better Homes and Gardens.

WOOD ™

FINISHING TECHNIQUES

YOU CAN USE

WE CARE!

All of us at Meredith® Books are dedicated to giving you the
information and ideas you need to create beautiful and useful
woodworking projects. We guarantee your satisfaction with this
book for as long as you own it. We also welcome your comments
and suggestions. Please write us at Meredith® Books, BB-117,
1100 Walnut St., Des Moines, IA 50309-3400.

A **WOOD**™ **BOOK**
Published by Meredith® Books

MEREDITH® BOOKS
President, Book Group: Joseph J. Ward
Vice President and Editorial Director: Elizabeth P. Rice
Executive Editor: Connie Schrader
Art Director: Ernest Shelton
Prepress Production Manager: Randall Yontz

WOOD® MAGAZINE
President, Magazine Group: William T. Kerr
Editor: Larry Clayton

FINISHING TECHNIQUES YOU CAN USE
Produced by Roundtable Press, Inc.
Directors: Susan E. Meyer, Marsha Melnick
Senior Editors: Sue Heinemann, Marisa Bulzone
Managing Editor: Ross L. Horowitz
Graphic Designer: Leah Lococo
Design Assistant: Leslie Goldman
Art Assistant: Ahmad Mallah
Copy Assistant: Amy Handy

For Meredith® Books
Editorial Project Manager/Assistant Art Director: Tom Wegner
Contributing Techniques Editor: Bill Krier
Contributing Outline Editor: David A. Kirchner

Special thanks to Khristy Benoit

PREPPING TIPS AND TECHNIQUES

A well-prepared surface is the key to a finishing job with professional results. From choosing the right strippers, sanders, and abrasives, to cleanup techniques that really make a difference, learn the right ways of preparing wood for a smooth, beautiful, and lasting finish.

OFF WITH THE OLD

The moment of truth in any refinishing project comes near the beginning, when you lift off the old finish and get your first good look at the bare wood underneath. Look at what we found here!

What's the best way to give the heave-ho to a tired old finish? The answer almost always is with a chemical that interacts with the finish's vehicle, be it the resins in shellac, lacquer, or varnish, or the linseed oil in many paints. Once the vehicle liquefies, you then *gently* lift it off with steel wool, a putty knife, scraper, or, in some cases, with a stream of water from a hose.

The key to success in any furniture stripping project lies with the chemical you choose to do the job, and in applying it properly. Safety is a big factor, too—you're working with toxic substances that can irritate the skin, eyes, and lungs (particularly methylene chloride). Many of the products are highly flammable as well.

Commercial paint and varnish removers will soften just about any finish, but before you rush out to buy a gallon or two, take a few minutes to analyze just what you're dealing with.

First, what exactly is the old finish? Paint is obvious, but you may need to give clear finishes a couple of simple tests. Dab an area with denatured alcohol. If the finish liquefies, it's shellac (you'll know immediately). If it gets soft but doesn't dissolve, it's most likely a mixture of shellac and lacquer.

Now test with lacquer thinner; if it liquefies, the finish is lacquer. To strip shellac and lacquer, you don't need a commercial remover. Instead, just use the appropriate solvent, mixing alcohol and lacquer thinner 50–50 to dissolve a combination shellac/lacquer finish.

If the piece is more than 150 years old and has been painted, you might want to try a third test, this time with ammonia. If ammonia liquefies the finish, it's milk paint, and only ammonia will take it off. Think long and hard, however, about whether you want to remove milk paint. Much of the value of older painted furniture depends on its having the original finish. What's more, ammonia is a dangerous, highly toxic chemical to be working with.

Choose your weapons and prepare for battle!

Once you've ruled out shellac, lacquer, and milk paint, you can stop testing. Regardless of what the finish might be—varnish, polyurethane, or whatever—you're going to have to invest in a commercial paint and varnish remover.

The chart on *the following page* compares liquid, semipaste, heavy-paste, and water-rinse strippers, as well as denatured alcohol and lacquer thinner. For information on new dibasic ester (DBE)-based and N-methyl pyrrolidone (NMP) removers, see *page 14*.

Stripping formulas vary according to the maker and to the jobs they do best. Methylene chloride is the highly toxic substance in most strippers that eats away the old finish. It evaporates rapidly, so strippers also contain waxy additives to slow evaporation. The amount of these additives determines how effective—and also how costly—a stripper will be. In general, the harder the finish and the more layers underneath, the more potent the stripper required and the more likely that you'll need several applications.

Major manufacturers often offer several, if not all, of the strippers, so if you're not having much luck with, say, a semipaste, step up to a heavy-paste remover from the same manufacturer. Don't mix brands, though; some formulations can neutralize others.

Water-rinse strippers are a good all-around choice. They have lots to recommend themselves, with a few drawbacks. Instead of only being able to scrape off the softened finish, you may be able to wash it away with a wet sponge, brush, or steel wool or, better yet, hose it off.

Water-rinse strippers are very effective, easy to use, and nonflammable. Because you're literally floating away the finish, you run almost no risk of gouging the wood. The only trouble is, you really have to flood the surface, and water can stain some woods and peel off veneers. If you decide to use a water-rinse stripper, be sure to dry the wood thoroughly with a soft towel afterward and let the piece air dry for several days.

continued

OFF WITH THE OLD
continued

Type	Use On	Safety	How To Apply
Liquid stripper	Works best on large horizontal surfaces such as tabletops.	Toxic and flammable	Pat on with a brush, let stand for about 15 minutes, and lift off sludge with a putty knife. Liquid stripper evaporates rapidly.
Semipaste stripper	Removes most paints and varnishes, but not effective on polyurethane or epoxy-based finishes.	Some are non-toxic and non-flammable	Pat on with a brush, let stand, lift off with a putty knife.
Heavy-paste stripper	Effective with many layers of paint, varnish, epoxy, polyurethane, and marine finishes.	Toxic but non-flammable	Pat on, let stand, lift off.
Water-rinse stripper	Removes just about any finish but don't use on veneers or inlays.	Nontoxic and non flammable	Brush on, let stand, then wash off with a hose or sponge. Dry off as quickly as possible.
Denatured alcohol	Shellac. Alcohol can also remove shellac sealers under other finishes such as varnish.	Toxic and flammable	Brush on, then rub off immediately with steel wool. Work quickly, in small sections at a time; alcohol evaporates quickly.
Lacquer thinner	Lacquer. Mixed 50–50 with alcohol, thinner will remove combination shellac and lacquer finishes.	Toxic and flammable	As with alcohol, brush on and rub off with steel wool, doing small sections at a time.

Step by step: Brush it on, wipe it off, and clean 'er up

Believe it or not, furniture stripping can be fun, albeit messy, as we discovered when we unmasked the beautiful Honduras mahogany occasional table pictured on *page 5*. The whole process took just a couple hours in our shop, start to finish (see photos, *opposite*).

Chemicals strong enough to dissolve layers of old paint and varnish are toxic, and most are flammable as well, so be careful and protect yourself (see tips, on *page 8*). Methylene chloride fumes pose the biggest health hazard in many strippers: At this writing, several federal agencies are weighing the possibility of restricting its use.

Set up in an open, well-ventilated place, such as a garage, driveway, or patio, but avoid direct sunlight: Heat can quickly dry out stripping agents and impede their effectiveness. If you must work in a basement or other location where ventilation is not especially good, place a fan near floor level. Fumes, which can be highly explosive, tend to settle.

Protect the floor by first spreading out a plastic drop cloth, then laying several thicknesses of newspapers on top. Remove layers of paper periodically as they become saturated with stripper sludge. Cat-box filler, sawdust, and/or wood shavings spread over the papers will help absorb sludge.

Before applying stripper, remove all hardware, handles, knobs, and latches. Drop them in a can partially filled with stripper, and cap it. You needn't totally cover the hardware; the fumes will soften the finish. When you have your piece stripped, grime will wash away.

Now, pour a small quantity of stripper into a metal—not plastic or glass—container. Use old or cheap synthetic brushes and plan to throw them away at the end of the day.

1. (See photo, *opposite*.) Brush on a generous amount of stripper in one direction only, and don't go back over an area unless the stripper appears to be drying out immediately. Apply stripper to top surfaces unless you want to test a small, less visible area first. You may want to remove the top entirely in order to treat both sides of the piece—an important precaution if you want to avoid warpage that can occur if only one side is treated.

2. As you reach the bottom of the piece, put its legs one at a time in a shallow pan to catch any stripper runoff. The time a stripper takes to do its job depends on the product and the old finishes. After the surface begins to wrinkle (up to about 15 minutes, usually), lightly test a small section with a putty knife. If the whole mess comes right off, the stripper has completed its job. If some areas seem to hold fast or pull at the putty knife, wait another 15 minutes or so and try again. If you still don't see bare wood, brush on more stripper.

Remove the stripper sludge from flat surfaces with a wooden or heavy-duty plastic scraper, a spatula, or a putty knife (round the corners to avoid gouging). Hold the scraper at a shallow angle to the surface and aim to *lift*, not scrape off the sludge (see photo, *page 4*). Avoid permanent damage from scratching or cutting into the wood fibers with your scraper.

At this point you'll probably be delighted at how effortlessly sludge slides off flat surfaces. Turnings, carvings, and crevices require more patience and ingenuity, however. The first thing you may discover is that remover doesn't cling well to vertical and cylindrical surfaces.

A trick that works for one refinisher we know is to apply stripper; then immediately wrap the part with aluminum foil; the foil helps hold remover against the finish and also retards evaporation. There's also a stripper-impregnated fiber product that does the same job in one step. Now for the nooks and crannies.

continued

1

2

3

4

5

6

7

8

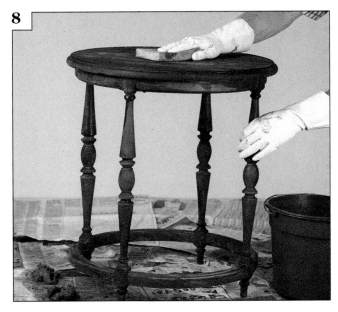

OFF WITH THE OLD
continued

3. Remove sludge from rounded and turned surfaces with medium-fine steel wool, not a scraper; scraping could flatten the wood.

4. To clean out the crevices in turnings, loop a piece of heavy string or thin hemp rope around them and pull it back and forth shoeshine fashion. For slight tapers, make a thick rope of steel wool and use it the same way.

5. Use a toothpick to clean out tight corners, beads, and joints. Carvings are especially tricky, because finish tends to build up in them and because you don't want to damage these important decorative elements.

6. You can also use a toothbrush in tight spots. A word to the wise: With delicate carvings (this piece had none), don't use metal tools that could gouge the wood.

7. After you've removed all the sludge, scrub the stripped piece with sawdust, then a sponge, rag, or with fine steel wool soaked in water or in the solvent recommended by the stripper's maker. Lacquer thinner is the most common. This washdown not only removes any remaining finish, it also neutralizes and flushes away stripper chemicals. If you find clear streaks that seem embedded in the grain, the wood was probably sealed with shellac, which can be removed by rubbing with steel wool dabbed in denatured alcohol.

8. Our final step with any project is a washdown with a household cleaner solution like Spic 'n Span or Soilax. Rinse several times, changing water if necessary to avoid discoloring the piece (notice how dark the newly lifted stain appears in our final photo).

Tips on working safely with strippers

Once you've seen what a chemical stripper can do to paint or varnish, you'll want to keep it away from your skin. Wear old clothes, long sleeves, and rubber gloves, and *protect your eyes with safety goggles.* Fumes from MC strippers can irritate eyes; cause headaches; and, after prolonged exposure, damage throat and lung membranes. Always work in a well-ventilated place and take a fresh-air break every 10 minutes or so. Also keep these pointers in mind:

• Never smoke in a space where stripper 's being used, and avoid any areas near an open flame, such as a furnace pilot light.

• Don't drink beverages containing alcohol before or while using a stripper. Not only can alcohol affect your judgment, it may make you more sensitive to fumes.

• Keep children and pets completely out of the area.

• If stripper accidentally splashes onto your skin, wash it off immediately with cool, soapy water.

• Don't save old brushes or partially filled jars or coffee cans of stripper. Seal the manufacturer's can (virtually all have childproof caps) and store it in a cool, safe place.

• Dispose of sludge-covered newspapers and other stripping residue as soon as you're finished with a job. Bag them in a plastic garbage bag, seal it well, and keep it away from heat (poke a few holes in the bag for ventilation). Spontaneous combustion can result if trash containing stripper lies around very long.

• Read your product's instructions carefully. Not all strippers work alike.

Nonchemical ways to remove paint and varnish

Usually, commercial paint and varnish removers offer the best way to strip furniture, but there are a couple of other methods for getting rid of an old finish, and occasionally they make better sense.

Scraping. Artisans who restore pieces for museums often prefer to shave off old finishes with cabinet scrapers, rather than risk subjecting valuable furniture to chemicals and lifting out the original stain, filler, or sealer. Also, some strippers break down old glues, causing joints to weaken. Obviously this process requires highly skilled hands and a lot of patience.

There is, however, one instance when you might want to consider scraping—with an old, badly cracked, flaking, dried out finish. When you can already see a lot of bare wood, especially on pieces such as outdoor furniture that have been exposed to the elements, stripper won't do a very good job because most of the vehicle, which stripper is formulated to liquefy, has already worn off. Fortunately, without a vehicle, the pigment has only a very weak grip on the wood, making it fairly easy to scrape away.

To scrape off a finish, use a cabinet scraper or a pull scraper, working always in one direction with the grain and held at a low angle. Keep a burr on the edge and rub in one direction—toward you. You are in essence shaving off the finish, but you don't want to cut the wood underneath.

Melting. Heat from a propane torch or an electric paint remover offers another, although risky, way to strip away an old finish. With a torch, you use a spreader tip and play the flame over the finish until it begins to buckle and lift, then scrape it off. With an electric paint remover, you hold it close to the surface until the finish softens, then you scrape.

Torching can easily scorch wood, or even set it on fire. Electric paint removers work only on large flat or gently curved surfaces. Both are more appropriate for large expanses of woodwork, siding, or paneling than they are for furniture.

GET SMOOTH RESULTS FROM YOUR BELT SANDER

A belt sander makes fast work of smoothing down rough stock. But if you're not careful, you can end up with ridges and gouges that seem to take forever to sand away. Here's how to do a perfect job every time.

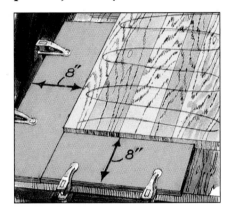

1. Belt sanders cut aggressively, so you've got to secure the workpiece to the bench before you start. Try this method: Clamp short, narrow stock in a vise, so it projects about ¼" above the clamp jaws.

To secure wide stock, clamp 6"- to 8"-wide plywood stops where shown on the drawing *above*. Again, you want the top surface of the workpiece to project above the stop strips so they don't interfere with the sander.

An alternative method is adhering the workpiece to the work surface with double-faced carpet tape. If you don't mind sanding away the tape residue, you can save time and clamping materials this way.

Using a pencil, draw a wavy line across the surface of the stock, as shown on the drawing. This provides you with a visual reference while sanding—after you've completely sanded away the mark, it's time to switch to a finer-grit paper.

2. Starting with 120-grit sandpaper, set the sander on the

stock midway between both ends as shown in the drawing *above*. Keep the sander perfectly flat to the wood surface when you turn it on. Hold the sander at a 15° to 20° angle to the direction you're sanding. Belt-sand up and down the length of the stock, moving to the right about 1" at the end of each pass. Let the machine's weight do the work.

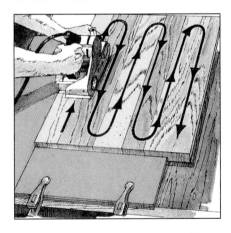

3. After you've sanded away the wavy line, switch to a finer-grit belt. Draw a second wavy line, and make straight passes, holding the machine parallel to the grain as shown *above*. Move to the right about 1" after each pass. When the pencil line vanishes again, switch to a finer grit for finish sanding.

4. No matter how carefully you sand, there's always the chance that

you'll accidentally gouge the wood. So, each time you finish sanding with a particular grit, check your work before moving to the next grit. We suggest you clamp a small light to your bench, as shown *above*, so that it illuminates the stock from a low angle. By standing behind the light and sighting down the length of the wood, you'll be able to see the slightest gouges.

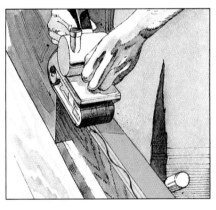

5. Sanding a narrow board or edge can be especially difficult because the sander tends to rock from side to side, rounding over the corners. Here's how to keep the corners sharp: Clamp a piece of scrap, called a *ledger,* to one side of the board (align both surfaces). Make the combined width of the ledger and board approximately equal to the width of the sanding belt. Draw a wavy line on the board and sand it, following the steps *above*.

TIME-TESTED STRATEGIES FOR REMOVING WOOD FINISHES

Knowing a few tricks of the trade can make a difference between a finish-removal job that goes bust, and one that reaps you great rewards.

1. Make safety a prime concern

Despite the advent of so-called "safe" finish removers in the past couple of years, most finishers still depend largely on methylene chloride-based formulations. That's because they need the most quick-acting, effective, and economical chemical available. But, using these powerful solvents does require that you carefully follow the safety precautions spelled out on product containers, such as wearing chemical-resistant gloves and goggles. It also pays to do the following:

• **Use a fan to expel air from your work area,** and open windows on the side of the room opposite the fan to provide cross-ventilation. Vapors of methylene chloride are heavier than air, so place your fan on the floor, not in a window.

• **Take frequent breaks.** If you experience dizziness, drowsiness, an inability to concentrate, or blurred vision, then you've overexposed yourself to the fumes.

• **Methylene chloride will irritate your skin,** so keep a bucket of soapy water on hand in case you accidentally come in contact with the chemical. These finish removers contain a wax for slowing evaporation; the soap cuts through the wax so the water can flush away the methylene chloride from your skin.

2. Proper application saves you headaches down the road

It doesn't pay to skimp when applying finish removers, so lay down a thick coating in accordance

with the product's instructions. Lay the remover on with an old nylon brush, and apply it in one direction only—don't go back over the remover with your brush to even it out. Restroking the chemical will disturb the wax skin that holds in the methylene chloride.

Never allow the finish remover to dry out, and be sure to do your project in manageable sections. Whatever surface you work on,

cover the entire area with remover for even coloration. If you strip half of a tabletop one day, and strip the other half another day, you may wind up with slightly different colors on the two halves, and a third color where the two applications overlapped.

If a drip of remover accidentally lands on an adjoining area, wipe it up immediately. Otherwise, the drip may show up as a light or dark area later.

3. Be gentle in your approach

If removing a finish makes you perspire, you're working too hard. Instead, let the finish remover do the hard work by leaving it on the project for all of the manufacturer's recommended time. After this period passes, the finish should slide off the workpiece with little effort on your part. Multiple layers of finish may require you to leave the finish remover in place for longer periods than recommended. Never force the finish from the surface with a scraper or putty knife—you may scratch or dent the wood fibers.

4. How to get out of tight spots

Okay, so you've stripped the flat surfaces of your project. Now comes the tricky part—getting the finish out of tight areas such as corners, turnings, and moldings. Here's some sound advice:

• Pry stubborn bits of finishes from intricate areas with sharpened dowels or toothpicks. Never use metal picks; they can damage wood.

• For help in pulling finishes out of nooks, crannies, and open grain, apply wood shavings soaked in finish remover. After allowing the finish remover to work, brush away the shavings.

• To get finish residue out from tight spots in turnings, use a coarse string or twine, much the way you use dental floss to clean your teeth.

5. How to cope with dark spots in oak surfaces

When water comes in contact with the naturally occurring tannic acid in oak over a long period of time, it results in a dark spot on the surface of the wood. These dark spots often pop up as crescent marks on tabletops where a wet glass or vase once stood.

Sometimes the spots appear where iron hardware contacted the surface.

If sanding doesn't remove these marks, treat the entire surface with a solution of 3 tablespoons of oxalic-acid crystals in 8 ounces of water. For a mail-order source of oxalic acid, see the Buying Guide *below right.* The acid solution will pull the dark stains from the wood grain. Next, you must neutralize the surface with a solution of 1 teaspoon of baking soda in 8 ounces of water.

6. Stubborn finishes: Wrap 'em up

Especially tough or thick finishes may not soften before the finish remover dries out. At these times, give the remover a helping hand by placing kitchen-variety plastic wrapping over the finish remover. This may be a little messy, but it seals in the methylene-chloride vapors and gives them time to work.

7. Put the heat on painted surfaces

Nothing removes thick layers of paint faster than a heat gun. This tool works well on large, flat surfaces such as doors or tabletops. (We do not recommend heat guns for use on fine furniture or delicate workpieces.) For best results, follow these pointers:

• Don't burn your hand or the workpiece. Burns in wood require lots of sanding for removal, so keep the heat gun moving at a steady rate to prevent scorching.

• As the heat gun softens the paint, quickly scrape away the residue with a putty knife before the finish cools and hardens. As with chemical strippers, never force the paint from the surface, and

round the corners of the putty knife to prevent scratches.

• Work outdoors or in an indoor area that's well ventilated. Wear a respirator to protect you from the harmful fumes.

• After you remove most of the paint with a heat gun, follow with a chemical remover to thoroughly cleanse the surface.

8. Residue: It all comes out in the wash

After you remove the bulk of the remover/finish sludge, the residue that remains on the surface will dry in a hurry. Don't let it. If the residue dries, you may have to put more finish remover on the surface. So, quickly wash the area with either 0000 steel wool or a fine Scotch Brite pad soaked in lacquer thinner. Then, clean the surface with a rag. To get out the last traces of residue, wipe the surface with a rag soaked in lacquer thinner.

Manufacturers of some products recommend that you clean up the residue with water. We've found that water leaves a fuzzy surface that adds to your sanding work. However, with dibasic ester (DBE)-based finish removers, such as 3M's Safest Stripper, you have no choice. You must clean up these with water. Since DBE solutions contain water, never use steel wool with these products (or you may get rust stains).

Buying Guide

• **Oxalic acid.** A 10-pound box of crystals. For current prices, contact Minuteman, P.O. Box 8, Waterloo, WI 53594, or call 800-733-1776

GETTING UNDER THE SURFACE OF TODAY'S FINISH REMOVERS

If you've gone shopping for a finish remover lately, you know how confusing the experience can be. Most container labels reveal little about how effectively the product removes a specific finish, how easy it is to apply and clean up, or how quickly it works. To find out the answers to these important questions, read on.

Formulators of finish-removal products have been doing quite a juggling act lately. Not long ago, these manufacturers had to be concerned only about putting out products that performed well and were affordable. Today, however, there is a growing public awareness of the health hazards associated with some of the chemicals in paint-and-varnish removers. This heightened concern has added safety to the factors manufacturers must juggle. The result, for consumers, has been the introduction of a dizzying array of products containing chemicals not previously seen in furniture-refinishing formulas. However, these so-called "safe" products have drawbacks of their own. Some types work slowly (overnight or longer) and others carry a relatively high price tag.

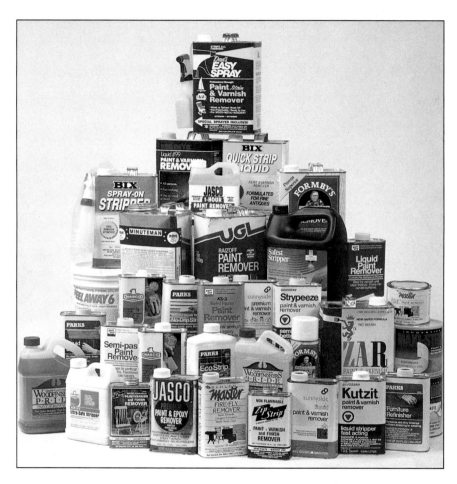

First, let's get to the bottom of the safety issue

Until recently, removing the finish from a piece of furniture meant you had to choose among finish removers containing powerful solvents such as methylene chloride (MC) or acetone, toluene, and methanol (ATM). Another option was caustic alkalines (CAs), otherwise known as lye.

These tried-and-true chemicals work quickly and effectively, but may pose threats to your health if not handled properly. For example, the highly flammable vapors released by ATMs can cause dizziness, headaches, and possibly nerve damage after extended exposure. Using CAs can result in severe skin and eye damage, and can actually harm a project if misused. For this reason, removers containing CAs have been reserved largely for professional use.

As nasty as these solvents sound, even more controversy swirls around the safety of MC. Although nonflammable, this chemical was proved to cause cancer in mice,

and it also has been linked to heart and kidney ailments. However, MC manufacturers point out that the chemical caused cancer only after the mice inhaled air containing 4,000 parts per million of MC. Cancer was not found in rats or hamsters at similar exposure levels.

Nevertheless, these findings prompted several companies to manufacture so-called safe strippers, containing the chemicals N-methyl pyrrolidone (NMP) or dibasic esters (DBE). Unlike other finish removers, these products release little odor. Although we did not feel any ill effects from their vapors during our tests, the material safety data sheets for some of the NMP products list dizziness and nausea as possible side effects of extended inhalation.

What do these considerations mean to you? Any of these chemicals can be used safely, but some require you to take more precautions than others. So, your choice of product depends on how much effort you want to expend in safe handling. The chart on the *following page* shows, among other things, the safety precautions required for each of the six types of finish-removal products.

How to choose the type of stripper that's right for you

Okay, so safety is important, but there's a lot more to consider. Some of us can't wait all day for a finish remover to work. And for most woodworkers, price also matters. Since everybody has different requirements when it comes to price, safety, and performance, we've spelled out the key differences between the types of finish removers in the chart on the *following page.*

What our tests revealed

Of all the testing we've conducted in the *WOOD®* magazine shop, sampling finish removers proved to be one of our toughest chores ever. But now that all of the testing is behind us, we feel confident that we know what type of product to choose for our next refinishing project. As you will see, the situation sometimes determines your product choice.

•**Methylene chloride (MC) finish removers: A hard-working bunch**. In our tests, the MC products proved themselves tops in

Sprayable MC finish removers deliver great results and convenience. To prevent running, the formulations gel on contact with finished surfaces.

stripping effectiveness. We especially liked the spray-on formulations for their ease of application. As shown in the photo *above,* you can apply a uniform layer of remover by simply pumping the spray bottle included with the spray-on products. We didn't even find it necessary to don our rubber gloves until we cleaned up the removers.

Besides offering convenience, this system eliminates a serious drawback of brush-on finish removers. The manufacturers' directions listed on these products state that you should brush the remover as little as possible and in only one direction. This way, you don't disturb the waxy skin that forms on top of the finish remover to prevent the evaporation of solvents. We found brush-on MC removers difficult to apply properly, especially on vertical, turned, and carved surfaces. No matter how hard we tried, we could not apply the strippers uniformly; we often wound up with thin areas that required a second coating.

Although the sprayable products have a liquid consistency, they thicken when they come in contact with a finished surface. This property helps them cling to vertical surfaces better than most other MC and ATM strippers.

Among the brushable MC products, we found differences in ease of cleanup. Some of them came out of their containers in slimy globs that made cleanup exasperating. Globs like the one in the photo on *page 15* slithered all over the work surface.

Manufacturers of some of the MC-based finish removers claim that you can clean up their products with water. Although water works with these products, we didn't find this to be an advantage. In our tests, washing the workpiece surface with water made it slightly fuzzy. For this reason, we suggest washing away the residue of nearly all stripping products with a rag soaked in lacquer
continued

GETTING UNDER THE SURFACE OF TODAY'S FINISH REMOVERS
continued

HOW THE SIX TYPES OF FINISH REMOVERS STACK UP

PRODUCT TYPE	ADVANTAGES	DISADVANTAGES	PRECAUTIONS YOU NEED TO TAKE
Methylene Chloride (MC)-based finish removers (products containing more than 70 percent MC)	The strongest and quickest removers available. Powerful enough to remove even polyurethanes and epoxy paints. Nonflammable. Some brands available in convenient sprays.	MC has caused cancer in certain laboratory animals. Also has been linked to heart and kidney ailments. Some brands have globs that make cleanup difficult.	
Acetone, Toluene, Methanol (ATM)-based finish removers	Remove most paints and clear finishes quickly. Inexpensive. Liquid forms work well for dissolving finishes in small crevices. Easy cleanup.	Highly flammable. Vapors can cause headaches and dizziness. Some brands evaporate quickly, requiring you to work fast. You need to scrub work surface vigorously for products to perform.	
MC/ATM finish removers (less than 70 percent MC, with ATM for balance of product)	Not as strong as MC-based products, but more effective than ATM finish removers. ATMs bring down the price.	Flammable. Products have all the safety hazards of MC and ATM formulations.	
N-Methyl Pyrrolidone (NMP)-based finish removers	Fastest of the "safe" products (15 minutes to more than 1 hour, depending on the concentration of NMP). Slight odor. Nonflammable.	Expensive (cost nearly twice as much as MC removers). Can cause dizziness and nausea after prolonged exposure.	
Dibasic Ester (DBE)-based finish removers	Least expensive of the "safe" products (about the same cost as MC-based removers). Almost no odor. Cling well to vertical surfaces. Nonflammable.	Work slowly (take 12-24 hours). Leave wood surface slightly fuzzy.	
Caustic Alkalines (CA)	Effective on multiple layers of enamel paint. Nonflammable.	Can cause severe skin burns. Darkens wood, so you must apply paint over treated surfaces.	

Eye protection   Approved respirator   Adequate ventilation   Rubber gloves   Do not use near an open flame

thinner. (DBE formulations require a water rinse.)

• **Acetone, toluene, methanol (ATM) formulations: A smart choice at times.** Sometimes, MC strippers, the workhorses of our tests, may have more muscle than you need. An ATM or MC/ATM stripper may remove the finish just fine—and save you a little money. However, remember that these products are flammable; also, they require vigorous scrubbing with a plastic scouring pad or steel wool in order to do their work. Some of them evaporate quickly, so you need to work quickly. On the plus side, ATM-only products clean up in a flash.

• **N-methyl pyrrolidone (NMP) removers: Good stuff if you can afford them.** Although the NMP finish removers work more slowly than MC and ATM products, you should give them serious consideration. Here's why. You get the same results if you wait just a few minutes longer— and you avoid noxious fumes in

Some of the finish removers have slimy globs that make even application and quick cleanup a frustrating and nearly impossible chore.

the process. Because of the expense of NMP, manufacturers vary the concentration of this chemical in an attempt to hold down the cost of the product. That's why some brands work more effectively than others.

• **Dibasic ester-based products: Safe but slow.** Of all the tested products, the DBE finish removers were the most pleasant to use—if you don't mind waiting 12 to 24 hours for results. We did notice that these strippers tended to fuzz the wood surface slightly. So, you need to sand the workpiece lightly before applying new finish.

These products also cause metals to rust, so you must avoid steel wool when scrubbing the work surface. Instead, use plastic scouring pads like the ones made for use with nonstick kitchenware. Since these pads do not quickly load up with finish residue the way steel wool does, we prefer using them with all of the finish removers.

KNOW YOUR WOODWORKING ABRASIVES

If you think "abrasives" means sandpaper and steel wool, you've only scratched the surface. With the large selection of products now available, you'll find it easier than ever to smooth your way to a fine finish.

Coated abrasives: Sandpaper and a whole lot more

Coated abrasives include products made up of abrasive minerals bonded to a backing material with a glue or resin bonding agent. Yes, they still come in the familiar sheets, disks, belts, and drums. But you'll also find them on other backings: cords, cloth strips, and sponge-backed blocks for sanding contoured surfaces and getting into tight places. Each form has its uses, as shown in the chart *below*. But no matter which form you choose, you also have to pick the right *abrasive minerals* and *grit sizes* to get the best results.

Four options in abrasive minerals

When selecting abrasive coatings, you can choose from two natural minerals (flint and garnet) and two manufactured ones (aluminum oxide, and silicon carbide).

1. Flint: Inexpensive, but no bargain!

Flint, the original sandpaper mineral, has been made practically obsolete. It breaks down easily and dulls more quickly than the other abrasive minerals. If you can find flint, it will be in sheet paper only. Our advice: Don't waste your money.

2. Garnet: A fast-cutting paper for hand sanding

Garnet remains the woodworker's favorite for most hand-sanding operations. This mineral fractures easily as you sand, producing extremely sharp edges—great for quickly removing material by hand. However, even the finest grit garnet papers don't leave quite as smooth

Abrasive minerals by color:
1. silicon carbide
2. aluminum oxide (coated with zinc stearate)
3. aluminum oxide (coarse)
4. aluminum oxide (fine)
5. garnet
6. flint

a surface as aluminum oxide or silicon carbide papers. For this reason, when hand-sanding hard woods, we generally use garnet papers up to 150-grit, then finish-sand with 220-grit aluminum oxide or silicon carbide paper.

Also, garnet won't hold up to the pressure exerted by power sanding machines nearly as well as aluminum oxide or zirconia alumina.

3. Aluminum oxide: An all-around performer

You'll find aluminum oxide available in more forms than any other abrasive mineral—sheets, disks, drums, sanding blocks, cords, and nonwoven finishing pads. The

Choosing the right abrasive for the job

Application	Tool/Product	Abrasive	Grit
Surfacing rough wood, fast stock removal	Surface sander; belt sander	Aluminum oxide	36–80
Rough-sanding mill marks, saw marks, defects, end grain	Orbital sander, belt sander, disk sander	Aluminum oxide, garnet	60–100
Smooth sanding	Orbital sander, disc sander, sheet sandpaper	Aluminum oxide, garnet, silicon carbide	120–320
	Sanding blocks, nonwoven pads	Aluminum oxide, silicon carbide	medium-fine
Sanding contours	Sanding drums, disks, flappers, cords, strips	Aluminum oxide, garnet, silicon carbide	80–320
	Sanding blocks, nonwoven pads	Aluminum oxide, silicon carbide	coarse-fine
Wet sanding, applying stains or oils, sanding between finish coats.	Sanding sheets nonwoven pads	Silicon carbide, aluminum oxide	240–600 fine-extra fine
	Steel wool		00–0000

light- to dark-brown, wedge-shaped particles resist fracturing, but aren't as sharp as garnet. This durability makes aluminum oxide good for power sanding, because machine speed compensates for its slower cutting properties. Use the finer grits (220, 320) for final dry sanding before applying the finish.

4. Silicon carbide: Use it for finish sanding, wet or dry

Silicon carbide particles have extremely hard, sharp edges that cut faster than aluminum oxide or garnet. We found that fine-grit silicon carbide sheets cut faster and last much longer than aluminum oxide. So, we prefer these for finish-sanding hardwoods by hand and, with a waterproof backing, for wet-sanding bare wood and finishes between coats (see *page 18*). But silicon carbide costs more than garnet or aluminum oxide, and it doesn't work quite as well as garnet for rough-sanding by hand. It also doesn't hold up as well as aluminum oxide for power sanding.

Grit sizes: Our recommendations

Grit number (or mesh number) refers to the particle size of the mineral used for the abrasive. The numbers range from 36-grit on coarse abrasive belts to 600-grit on very fine silicon carbide papers. However, the sanding products you'll most often use fall within the 60- to 220-grit range.

When sanding bare wood prior to finishing, you don't need to work your way through the full range of available grit sizes, especially if you use a power sander for some of the work. For instance, to smooth a flat surface, we usually start with a portable or stationary belt sander equipped with an 80- or 100-grit aluminum-oxide belt. Then, we switch to a finishing sander, using 150-grit or 180-grit garnet paper, then 220-grit aluminum oxide paper. The chart *opposite* lists the recommended abrasives and grit sizes for various sanding procedures.

Sand "paper" alternatives include foam sanding blocks (1–4), cloth-backed sanding strips (5), and abrasive cords and tapes (6). Use these products for sanding contoured surfaces and getting into tight spots.

Here's what we usually stock in the *WOOD®* shop:
• Sheet paper: garnet, 60-, 80-, 100-, 150-grit; aluminum oxide, 220-, 320-grit.
• Belts for portable belt sander: aluminum oxide, 60- 80-, 100-, 150-grit.
• Belts for stationary belt sander: aluminum oxide, 80- or 100-grit.
• 9" disks for stationary disk sander: 60-, 100-grit.
The above abrasives handle most of our sanding chores, so we try to keep a good supply on hand. We buy more specialized abrasive products as we need them.

Open-coat *vs.* closed-coat papers

Here's yet another decision to make. On closed-coat sandpapers, the abrasive mineral covers the entire surface. On open-coat papers, the mineral covers only 50–70 percent of the paper's surface, so they won't clog or fill up as quickly as closed-coat papers. We generally use open-coat paper on resinous softwoods and other woods that tend to "load up" or clog the paper; also for power sanding. Closed-coat paper cuts faster because it has more abrasive mineral on the surface, which makes it a better choice for most hand-sanding chores.

Manufacturers treat some of their silicon carbide and aluminum oxide papers with zinc stearate to keep them from loading up. The treatment also turns the paper off-white, as shown in the photo *opposite*. We like to use these papers in the finer grits for finish sanding.

Flexible abrasives for sanding contours

The following specialized sanding products will help you smooth out the curves and get into those hard-to-reach spots.

Foam sanding blocks have a backing of flexible sponge material with an aluminum oxide abrasive coating on one, two, or four sides. The palm-size blocks measure about 3" wide by 4" long by ½" to 2" thick. As shown in the photo *above,* the abrasive may be bonded directly to the pad (1), attached with a hook-and-pile fastener (2), or bonded to an intermediate fabric backing (3, 4). When the blocks clog up with sanding residue, just wash them in clean water and reuse.

We found that all of these blocks work well on flat and contoured surfaces, but are too flexible to use for a sharp edge or corner.

continued

KNOW YOUR WOODWORKING ABRASIVES
continued

Flapper-type sanders fit portable drills. They work well on the beads and coves of spindles and other turnings.

Inflatable drum sanders fit portable drills, drill presses, and lathes. You inflate them with an air pump.

Cloth-backed sanding strips, or *shop rolls* come in standard grit sizes from 40- to 240-grit You can buy the 50-yard rolls in 1", 1½", and 2" widths. They're great for hand-sanding contoured shapes, such as turned spindles. Keep a roll handy next to your lathe.

Abrasive cords get you into those tight spots that other sanding products won't reach. Made exclusively by the Mitchell Company, the aluminum-oxide-coated cloth cords come in widths from ⅟₁₆" to ¼", and standard grits from 120 to 200.

In addition to these products, you'll find two nifty power tool attachments for contour sanding—flap sanders and inflatable sanding drums (see photos *above*).

Specialty abrasives for a fine finish

The sanding process on bare wood usually ends with 220-grit sandpaper. Then you apply the finish of your choice. But in some cases, you may need an even smoother surface prior to applying the finish. In such situations, you can wet-sand with fine-grit wet/dry sandpapers, or

use steel wool or nonwoven finishing pads for final smoothing.

You also can use these products to smooth and level sealers and finishes between coats. We have found that the fine-grit finishing pads also work great for applying penetrating finishes, such as Danish oil or tung oil. (See photo *opposite*.)

Wet/dry sandpapers come in most of the standard grit sizes, though you'll usually use 220- to 600-grit papers for wet-sanding wood and finishes. These silicon carbide papers have a waterproof bonding agent and backing.

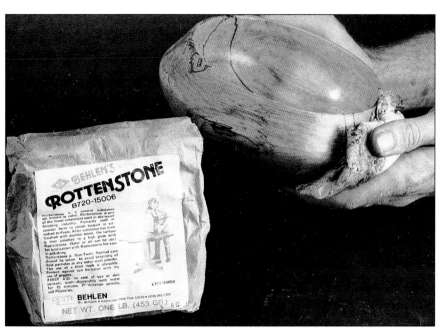

For a hand-rubbed finish, use lemon oil or paraffin oil and a felt cloth to rub out finishes with pumice and rottenstone.

Nonwoven finishing pads work great for smoothing wood while applying oil finishes; also for leveling hard finishes between coats.

Steel wool comes in seven grades, ranging from 3 (coarsest) to 0000 (finest). Use the coarser grades for removing chemical paint strippers during refinishing. Use the finer grades (00–0000) for smoothing contoured surfaces prior to applying a finish, and between finish coats.

Steel wool has always elicited two major complaints from woodworkers—it rusts, and it sheds tiny strands of steel, which you must then remove with a tack cloth.

To prevent rust, most manufacturers put a light coat of oil on the steel wool pads. This oil may

affect the adhesion or penetration of some stains and finishes. We suggest that you soak the pads in acetone or lacquer thinner to remove the oil before using them. High-quality steel wools have longer strands, so they won't shed quite as much as low-quality ones. Some are also oil-free.

Nonwoven finishing pads have the best qualities of wet/dry sandpaper and steel wool. The ¼"-thick nylon fiber pads easily conform to contoured surfaces, won't shed, and can be cut into various shapes and sizes. Most come impregnated with silicon carbide or aluminum oxide

powders in various grits, which are labeled *coarse* to *extra fine*.

We have found that these pads outlast steel wool and sandpaper.

Pumice and rottenstone have one purpose only—to rub out the topcoat of hard finishes, such as lacquer, varnish, and shellac. (Don't use them on oil finishes.) You mix these powdered abrasives with an oil lubricant, such as paraffin oil or lemon oil, and apply them with a felt pad. Pumice comes in coarse and fine grades. You start with the coarse grade, then go to the fine grade. If you want an even higher polish, follow up with rottenstone mixed with a lubricant.

SANDING SHORTCUTS

Ask any group of wood-workers what they like least about their craft, and we bet that most of them will vote for sanding. In fact, inventors and manufacturers from far and wide have devised one gadget after another to extract the pain out of this drudgery. For truly professional results, you need to get through the maze of abrasives and tools, know which ones to use for each job, and learn the tricks for putting these products to good use. And that's where this short course comes in.

Choosing the best abrasive for the job

If picking and choosing among today's abrasives rubs you the wrong way, just keep these buying points in mind:

• **You can select from three types of abrasives:** garnet, aluminum oxide, and silicon carbide. See the chart *opposite top,* for the advantages of each.

Garnet papers have naturally occurring minerals bonded to their surface. Because these grains have to be sifted, they're not consistent in size, so they abrade a surface less uniformly than man-made abrasives such as the following two varieties.

Besides having consistently sized particles, *aluminum-oxide* and *silicon-carbide* abrasives (both manmade) last longer because of their greater hardness. You can purchase the finer grades of these papers with a zinc-stearate coating that acts as a dry lubricant to reduce load-up of the surface with wood particles. Although this coating gives the abrasive a white coloring, don't assume that all white-colored abrasives have a zinc-stearate coating. For example, 3M colors its Stikit line of self-adhesive papers white for brand-identification purposes. To spot a zinc-stearate-coated product, look

ABRASIVE LANGUAGE: DEFINING THE CHOICES

ABRASIVE	SUGGESTED GRITS	ADVANTAGES	COMMENTS
Garnet	60, 80, 100, 150	• Has less tendency to burn end grain because garnet particles break down easily. • Low cost	• Garnet paper has a relatively short lifespan. • Available in paper-backed sheets only. • Grains of inconsistent size and color.
Aluminum Oxide	60, 80, 100, and 150 in belts. 60, 80, 100, 150, 220, and 320 in sheets	• Cuts faster, lasts longer, and has a more uniform surface than garnet abrasives.	• About the same price as garnet papers. • Grains of consistent size and color.
Aluminum Oxide with Zinc-Stearate Coating			• Zinc-stearate coating reduces load-up in fine grits.
Silicon Carbide	220–1500 in sheets	• Cuts faster and lasts longer than aluminum oxide. • Zinc-stearate coating reduces load-up. • Cuts faster, with less load-up, in glue-impregnated substances such as particleboard.	• Because of its higher cost, we prefer silicon-carbide abrasives for wet-sanding only. • Use with water for wet-sanding finish coats. • Grains of consistent size and color.

GETTING THE RIGHT GRIT

Grit	Heavy wood removal	Surface shaping	Surface flattening	Smoothing	Preparation for finish	Between finish coats
40						
60						
80						
100–120						
150–220						
320–600						

• **Know when to use an open-coat paper.** Most sandpapers have a closed coat, meaning that 100 percent of their surface is covered with abrasive grains. However, in some coarse grits you will find open-coat papers with only 70 percent grain coverage on their surfaces. This extra space between grains helps prevent clogging of the abrasive surface with wood fibers, especially when you work with softwoods.

Getting the most from sanding tools

Even the proper abrasives aren't of much help until you combine them with the correct tool. To help you along, we prepared the chart on the next two pages. In the *WOOD®* magazine shop, we make great use of the stationary belt/disc sander, portable belt sander, and our own hands for many sanding tasks. The following tips will help you better utilize these tools in your shop.

continued

for words such as "no-load," "no-fill," or "nonclogging." Although this coating adds a few cents to the cost of abrasives, we've found that it's money well spent.

• **Go with a grit to match the job.** An abrasive that's too coarse will lead to excessive scratch marks in your project's surface, and you will have to work hard to remove them. On the other hand, a sandpaper that's too fine for the job will clog with wood particles. So, check the chart *above* for the correct

succession of grits for your projects. In the *WOOD®* magazine shop, we typically true a surface with a 60-grit aluminum-oxide abrasive when necessary, then smooth the project with 120-grit garnet sandpaper. To prepare softwood surfaces for a finish, we sand with 150-grit garnet paper. Because hardwoods can take a more polished surface prior to finishing, we sand these woods with a succession of 150-grit paper and a 220-grit zinc-stearate-coated aluminum-oxide abrasive.

SANDING SHORTCUTS
continued

Stationary belt/disc sander tips

• **For perfectly flush half-lap joints,** cut the half laps ⅛₆" longer than the finished size, then sand them flush with a disc or vertical-belt sander as shown *below*.

Note: For this procedure, and the next two tips, the belt- or disc-sander table must be set at 90° to the abrasive surface.

Slightly long half-lap joints come perfectly flush with the aid of a disc or vertical-belt sander.

• **Fine-tune miter joints** on a vertical-belt or disc sander as shown *below*. Since few woodworkers can cut perfect miters every time, this method allows you to custom-match miters with complete control over stock removal. Because the disc moves faster near its rim than near its center, sand close to the center of

For slightly miscut miters, you can sand one of the pieces to fit the other exactly.

A BAKER'S DOZEN SANDING MACHINES: ONE FOR EVERY JOB

SANDER	PURPOSE	APPLICATIONS	SUGGESTED ABRASIVES
Sationary Belt (vertical) and Disc Sander	Rapid removal of stock on edges.	Sanding back to a line. Touching up miters and compound angles. Chamfering or rounding dowel ends.	36- to 120-grit cloth-backed aluminum oxide.
Stationary Belt (horizontal)	Rapid removal of stock on surfaces.	Flattening small areas of face grain. General smoothing and truing. Shaping. Use end of belt as free-hand drum sander.	36- to 120-grit cloth-backed aluminum oxide.
Stationary Edge Belt Sander	Rapid removal of stock on edges.	Smoothing edge grain. Sanding back to a line. Concave sanding on the open roller.	36- to 120-grit cloth-backed aluminum oxide
Stationary Strip Sander	Sanding small parts.	Metal sharpening. Inside edges and tight areas.	36- to 120-grit cloth-backed aluminum oxide.
Portable Belt Sander	Rapid removal of stock on large, flat surfaces.	Truing stock glued up for width. Lowering joints and edges to a uniform height. Mounted in accessory stands, these machines work as small stationary belt sanders.	60- to 120-grit cloth-backed aluminum oxide.
Finishing Sanders	Smoothing surfaces and protective finishes.	Final sanding. ¼-sheet (palm) sanders useful on small areas. ⅓- and ½-sheet models best for larger areas.	120- to 320-grit paper-backed aluminum oxide, garnet, or silicon carbide.

SANDER	PURPOSE	APPLICATIONS	SUGGESTED ABRASIVES
Random-Orbit Sanders (electric and pneumatic)	High-speed finish-sanding without swirl marks.	Flattening joints while leaving a smooth surface. Special pad available for contours.	80- to 320-grit paper and adhesive-backed aluminum oxide and silicon carbide.
Straightline Sanders (electric and pneumatic)	Sands with the grain.	Flattening high-low areas. Lowering joints and edges to a uniform height.	80- to 320-grit cloth-backed aluminum oxide and silicon carbide.
Flexible Disc Sander	Rapid stock removal on irregular surfaces.	Shaping, smoothing, and polishing small stock. Power-sanding bowls when chucked in a portable drill with lathe running. Various sizes available from 1–6".	36- to 400-grit cloth-, paper-, and adhesive-backed aluminum oxide and silicon carbide.
Flap Wheels	Conform to irregular surfaces.	Corrosion removal on tools and hardware. Sanding carvings and spindles.	60- to 180-grit cloth-backed aluminum oxide
Drum Sander	Sanding concave and convex edges to smooth, flowing shapes.	Sanding back to a line on curved, bandsawed edges.	60- to 150-grit cardboard-backed aluminum oxide.
Pneumatic (inflatable) Drum Sander	Smoothing and shaping of irregular surfaces	Smoothing carvings and intarsia parts. Fill drum bladder to varying pressures to change conformity of drum.	80- to 180-grit cloth-backed aluminum oxide
Hand Sander	Controllable truing and smoothing.	See page 67 for specialized sanding blocks to help you sand tight and irregular surfaces. Foam sanding blocks work well on rounded surfaces.	80- to 1,500-grit paper-, cloth- and adhesive-backed garnet, aluminum oxide, or silicon carbide.

the disc for slower, more controlled stock removal.

• **Perfectly shaped corners** result from marking a radius and then carefully sanding back to that line with a belt or disc as shown *below*. For maximum control, follow the illustrations *below*.

continued

Use a disc or vertical-belt sander to shape flowing convex curves.

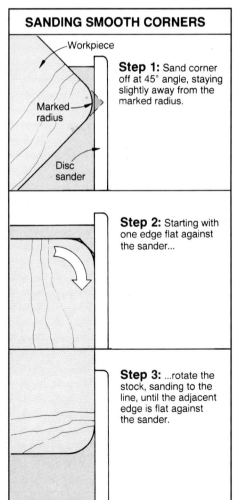

SANDING SMOOTH CORNERS

Step 1: Sand corner off at 45° angle, staying slightly away from the marked radius.

Step 2: Starting with one edge flat against the sander...

Step 3: ...rotate the stock, sanding to the line, until the adjacent edge is flat against the sander.

SANDING SHORTCUTS
continued

• **Make great-looking dowel chamfers** with the jig *below* clamped to your sander's table. With your sander running, place the dowel on the machine's table and hold it as shown *below*. Give the dowel at least one full rotation to sand a complete chamfer.

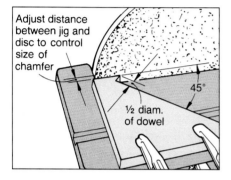

Adjust distance between jig and disc to control size of chamfer

45°

½ diam. of dowel

With the chamfering jig in place, spin the dowel until the chamfer is complete.

• **You can smooth small resawed stock** even if you don't own a thickness planer. With double-faced tape, attach a 1½"-thick block that's nearly as wide and long as the resawed piece to the face opposite the resawed surface. Then, lower the workpiece onto a moving horizontal belt as shown *below*. Be careful to keep

To smooth resawed stock, position it parallel to the sanding belt.

the workpiece parallel to the belt as the two surfaces make contact. Move the workpiece from side to side as you sand.

Portable belt sander pointers
• **For rapid stock removal with a portable belt sander,** hold the sander at approximately a 30° angle to the grain of the workpiece, and keep it cocked this way as you move the machine up and down the workpiece. This cross-grain sanding works fast, but leaves a rough surface.

• **To smooth surfaces,** work the belt sander as shown *below*. Hold the sander parallel to the grain, and keep the belt sander moving at all times. Work the sander in long paths that cover the full length of the workpiece. Minimize cross-grain movements.

• **For an evenly sanded surface,** don't bear down on the machine; let the weight of the sander do the work. And, be aware of how much of the belt is in contact with the workpiece. Otherwise, you may accidentally

miss the ends of the surface, or round over the edges by tipping the sander.

• **Drape the power cord over your shoulder** to keep it out of the way of the belt sander.

• **To check your work** for gouges and hollows, hold a light at a low angle to the surface.

Hand-sanding hints
• **Don't sell short the merits of hand sanding.** Power sanders save you plenty of time—no doubt about it—but a good, old-fashioned sanding block flattens a surface better than any machine. Also, a hand block gives you more control over those delicate situations such as gently rounding an edge. Around the *WOOD* magazine shop, we use a sanding block for the final smoothing of flat surfaces and between finish coats.

• **To save hand-sanding time,** you may want to invest a few dollars in a 3M Stikit sanding block such as the red one shown on *page 20*. We found these plastic blocks comfortable, and abrasive changes

Try to minimize cross-grain movements when smoothing a surface with a belt sander. Sand the full length of the workpiece and keep the machine moving.

take just a few seconds. To replace the sandpaper, you simply tear off the old abrasive and pull some fresh material from the built-in roll.

• **Custom-made sanding blocks** will save you loads of time when sanding tricky areas. As shown *below,* you can shape a variety of custom-made blocks to conform to most any smoothing task. Then, attach an adhesive-backed abrasive. Or, affix nonadhesive abrasives with glue or adhesive spray—just remember that the paper will be difficult to remove.

A few mistakes to avoid at all costs

Sometimes, what you *don't* do while sanding counts as much as what you *do* do. For help, keep these pointers in mind.

• **Don't let load-up bog you down.** Steve Martyr, a technical representative of 3M, estimates that most people toss away their sandpapers long before the abrasive particles wear out. The reason: Premature load-up of the abrasive with sanding dust. If you experience load-up early in the life of your abrasives, Steve suggests you switch to either a coarser grit or an open-coat abrasive, or try a zinc-stearate-coated product.

Also, remember to collect sanding dust from the work surface to avoid load-up. Occasionally stop and vacuum both the work surface and the bottom of the sander.

• **Sanders can be as dangerous as any other cutting machine in your shop,** so keep all guards in place. If you've ever accidentally touched a moving sanding belt, you know how fast abrasives can remove skin. Guards also protect you if a belt tears.

• **Sanding dust contributes to lung disease,** so opt for machines with dust-collection capabilities when you go shopping. In recent years, power-tool manufacturers have concentrated more and more on dust-collection in designing their tools. For instance, today you can buy finish sanders that draw dust through holes in the sandpaper, and portable belt sanders with vacuum attachments.

We strapped a furnace filter to a window fan with bungee cord for an inexpensive dust evacuator.

If your sanders don't have dust-collection ports and accessories, rig up your own clean-air aids. As shown *above,* you can attach a furnace filter to the air-drawing side of a window fan, then point the fan away from you as you work. This simple dust collector will move much of the airborne dust away from you, and capture some in the process. But, remember that even with dust-collection systems in place, it still pays to wear an approved respirator.

• **Don't accidentally mar your flat workpieces** by setting them on a bare workbench when sanding them with an orbital finish sander. Instead, place some kind of cushion, whether it's a piece of carpet pad, cardboard, or even a blanket, under the workpiece before finish-sanding it, as we did in the photo *above.* Otherwise, any debris on the surface of your workbench will transmit swirly marks and dents to the back side of your project.

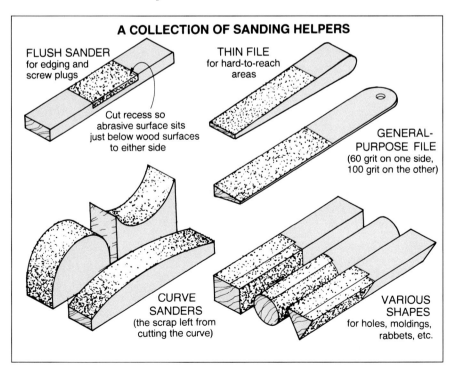

A COLLECTION OF SANDING HELPERS

FLUSH SANDER
for edging and screw plugs

Cut recess so abrasive surface sits just below wood surfaces to either side

THIN FILE
for hard-to-reach areas

GENERAL-PURPOSE FILE
(60 grit on one side, 100 grit on the other)

CURVE SANDERS
(the scrap left from cutting the curve)

VARIOUS SHAPES
for holes, moldings, rabbets, etc.

CABINET CLEANUP TRICKS

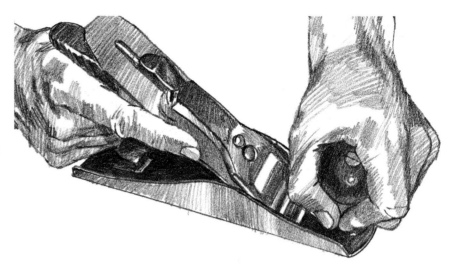

Contrary to what you might expect, savvy cabinetmakers don't put off sanding, scraping, and other cleanup work until after they have completed a project. The real pros plan for cleanup as part of the building process. Why? "Because it makes for a better end result, and when you're woodworking for hire, it's results that count," according to Jim Boelling, our *WOOD*® magazine project builder. And he should know because he's built more than his share of cabinets for us and for others during the past 20 years.

We followed Jim around the shop one afternoon not long ago, and listened and watched as he explained his tried-and-true techniques for prepping his work for the final finish. And, we weren't surprised when he gave us more than our money's worth in woodworking wisdom, which we'd now like to pass on to you.

Think cleanup first, then start building

Before cutting your first piece of wood for any project, anticipate which parts you will cut strong (oversized). Doing this provides you a small margin (about $\frac{1}{32}$") of waste material at joints. Why? You achieve a clean, flush joint by removing extra stock during the cleanup process.

The drawing *above right* shows how this "add, then subtract" method applies to a simple butt joint. "I cut the cabinet top (part A) so it will overlap the cabinet side (part B) by about the thickness of a dime after assembly. This margin enables you to clean up any saw marks and hardened glue squeezeout after assembly," Jim says. You can use this process throughout the cabinet construction process. For instance, it also pays to leave cabinet shelves about $\frac{1}{32}$"

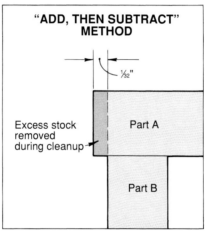

"ADD, THEN SUBTRACT" METHOD

$\frac{1}{32}$"

Excess stock removed during cleanup

Part A

Part B

wide before positioning them between two cabinet sides, then work the shelves flush.

It's especially important to leave yourself this margin if you're using thin-veneer plywood. For example, if you assemble the joint in the illustration *above* perfectly flush to begin with, you might end up sanding through the veneer on part B when you clean up part A.

How to make a molding flush with a surface

You can use the same "add, then subtract" method described *above* to work moldings flush to a cabinet top. The tools and techniques

shown in the sequence *opposite* also apply to other exposed joints.

First, cut all the mitered ends of the moldings and test them for fit. Then, glue molding onto the carcase approximately $\frac{1}{32}$" high to provide waste along the top edge of the cabinet as shown *below*. After the glue skins over (about 30 minutes), remove squeeze-out with a hand scraper. Then, use a smoothing plane to remove most of the waste, as shown in Step 1, *opposite*. "Stroke the plane at an angle toward the outside edge of the molding, and stop when the surfaces are almost flush," Jim advises.

Now, mark a pencil line on the cabinet top about $\frac{1}{4}$" away from the joint line and parallel to it. Next, with a sharp cabinet scraper, bring the joint flush and remove marks

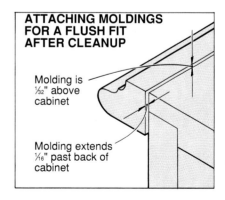

ATTACHING MOLDINGS FOR A FLUSH FIT AFTER CLEANUP

Molding is $\frac{1}{32}$" above cabinet

Molding extends $\frac{1}{16}$" past back of cabinet

Step 2: **Next, draw a pencil line running parallel to the joint and use a cabinet scraper until the line disappears.**

Step 1: **To work the molding flush with the cabinet top, start with a smoothing plane for fast stock removal.**

Step 3: **If you notice any minute imperfections after sanding, remove them with a hand scraper.**

Don't save the sanding for later

After cutting and milling all of your project pieces, clean up those parts and surfaces that would be difficult—or impossible—to do after assembly. Such parts might include the inside surfaces of the carcase and drawers, the edges of a raised-panel insert, and "plant-on" parts, such as moldings, decorative plaques, and filigrees.

continued

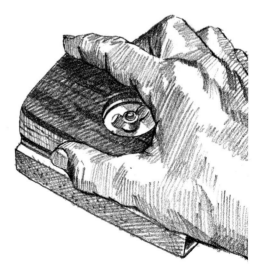

left by the plane as shown *above, top.* When the pencil line disappears, quit scraping.

Then, sand the joint smooth with a hardwood sanding block such as the one shown at *right*, using a succession of 180- and 220-grit papers. Sand with the grain of the cabinet top—not the molding—and

be careful not to round over the outside edge of the molding.

If minute sanding marks remain, follow up with a hand scraper as shown *above.* "With a scraper, you can quickly remove small scratches without introducing more sanding marks to the surface," Jim says.

CABINET CLEANUP TRICKS
continued

After scraping the beveled portion of a raised panel, we switched to a hardwood sanding block.

Sand convex surfaces by wrapping sandpaper around a felt pad.

As shown *above*, it pays to finish up the beveled edges of a raised panel before inserting it into a door frame. After using a hand scraper, sand with a hardwood sanding block to achieve a smooth, flat surface and crisp edges. Sand through a succession of 100-, 150-, and 220-grit papers. Because cross-grain edges require more sanding than other edges, clean up those first. Then, smooth the remaining two edges by lowering those to the profile of the cross-grain edges. Finally, smooth the flat surface of the panel with the same succession of grits. "It's also a good idea to stain the panel before inserting it into the frame," our resident pro adds. "If you stain the panel after it's in the frame, it may shrink across the grain, exposing a thin line of unstained wood along the edges."

A pro's procedure for sanding profiles

Whether you buy milled moldings or shape your own, the profile always needs touching up. First, sand all the concave (inward-curved) surfaces. To do this, wrap the sandpaper around a dowel that's long enough to fit comfortably in your hand (4–6") and that's equal to or slightly smaller than the radius of the surface being sanded as shown *opposite*. If you use a larger-diameter dowel, it will flatten the sharp profile edges and you'll lose the original molding shape.

Then, sand the convex (outward-curved) surfaces, wrapping the sandpaper around a piece of ¼"-thick sheet cork (available at many hardware and craft stores) or the rib of a felt chalkboard eraser as shown *above*.

Finally, clean up the flat shoulders (outside corners) and inside corners with a hardwood sanding block as shown *below*. Using the block ensures sharp, crisp lines.

Sand inside and outside corners with a hardwood sanding block to maintain sharp lines. The block should have square bottom corners for best results.

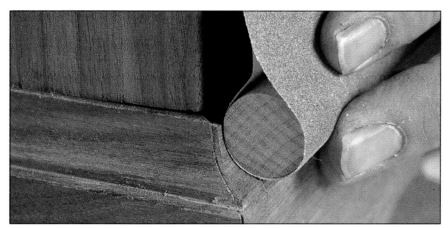

Hold the belt sander at an angle to avoid splintering the end of the molding.

Judicious sanding will give mismatched miters a matched look.

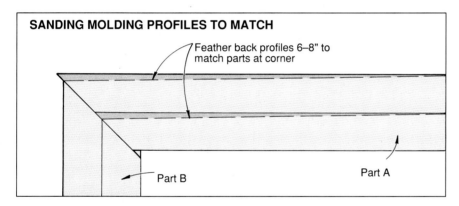

SANDING MOLDING PROFILES TO MATCH

Feather back profiles 6–8" to match parts at corner

Part B

Part A

How to manage a mismatched miter

It's not easy to cut and assemble a perfectly mitered joint. You can make exact and true cuts, but one or both of the pieces may creep out of alignment after you've glued and clamped them in position. Even an expert like Jim Boelling admits to the occasional mismatched miter. His advice: Take care of any problem miters before cleaning up molding profiles as described on the *previous page.* Here's how Jim handles troublesome miters.

First, determine if you can true-up the mitered corner without ruining the appearance of the project. "If the mismatch is, say,

more than $\frac{1}{16}$", remove the offending part before the glue dries and try again. You'll be happier in the long run," Jim advises.

To correct minor mismatches like the one shown *above, top,* follow the procedure illustrated *above.* First, sand off the projecting tip of Part A to make it flush with the outside edge of Part B. While sanding, gradually feather back the profile about 6" to 8" from the corner. Sand the length of pieces less than 8" long.

The finishing touches

Even if you put meticulous care into cleanup at every step, there are always some final touches to add. After cleaning up the molding

profiles, "break" (round over) all the sharp edges with fine sandpaper (220- or 320-grit). Hold the paper in your hand and use a light touch to remove a minimum of stock.

Finally, sand the back end of the molding (leave the molding $\frac{1}{16}$" long during construction as shown in the drawing on *page 26*) and back edges of the cabinet carcase flush with the hardboard back as shown *above.*

Once finished with the carcase, repeat the final cleanup process on the doors, drawers, and any other subassemblies, removing stock as required to ensure a proper fit. Then, vacuum or blow excess dust off the cabinet and wipe down all surfaces with a rag dampened in mineral spirits. This reveals any fine scratches, glue marks, or other minor imperfections you may have missed, and removes most sanding dust from the wood pores. After removing these blemishes, vacuum any remaining dust from the surface of the cabinet. Finally, apply the finish of your choice. You can bet your next project will have a professional appearance if you follow these proven suggestions.

CLEAR FINISHES

Let the natural beauty of the wood show through by adding a clear finish to the surface. You can choose from oils and pastes, water-based lacquers, polymers—even home brews—to give your piece the perfect finishing touch.

IN SEARCH OF THE PERFECT FINISH

Homemade finishes frequently stir up thoughts of secret ingredients and images of bubble, bubble, toil, and trouble. But, in fact, these finishes often outperform commercial concoctions. Here, San Diego furnituremaker and educator T.C. MacMichael demystifies his finishing process.

When T.C. MacMichael studied furniture design at Central Washington University in the mid-'70s, he experimented with various finishes. "I didn't like surface finishes such as lacquer and varnish—I felt I had to look through them to see the wood," he explains. "Oil finishes alone lacked the luminous quality I like. But, by working an oil and wax mixture into the wood, I achieved exactly the right finish."

T.C.'s finishing process includes three separate coats of Daly's SeaFin Teak Oil followed by two coats of a teak oil and beeswax mixture. Although each step requires a great deal of handwork, the results reflect the effort.

The finished piece not only has visual appeal, but it's a delight to touch. And, T.C.'s finish stands up to water and alcohol. In fact, this craftsman has so much confidence in his finishing process that he not only applies it to all his custom furniture, he also *teaches* the technique at San Diego State University, where he heads the furniture design program.

Setting up for teak oil

According to Kyle Peterson, factory sales representative for Daly's, their SeaFin Teak Oil contains tung oil, phenolic (plastic) resins, and dryers. Daly chemists formulated the finish for marine use. Today, though, it is widely applied to furniture, and for good reason. T.C. has discovered that the teak oil he uses protects the natural

color of the wood—such as the orange of padauk that traditionally darkens rather quickly—far longer than any other oil.

T.C. has the following supplies on hand when he starts a finishing project (see photo, on *page 32)* plenty of paper towels, 0000 steel wool, cheesecloth, clean cotton cloths, 400–600-grit wet/dry sandpaper, SeaFin Teak Oil, and beeswax. "The beeswax works easier than carnuba, and the results are equal," T.C. notes.

Step-by-step to a glowing finish

1. In preparation for finishing, T.C. sands all surfaces smooth with 220-grit paper, then blows off the sanding dust with compressed air or wipes it clean with a tack cloth. He next uses a soft cloth to flood the surface heavily with the first of three coats of plain teak oil. While the

wood is wet, T.C. sands with the grain with 400-grit wet/dry paper.

2. After a five-minute wait, T.C. removes all traces of oil on the wood's surface with soft cloths or paper towels. "When I finish porous woods, such as oak, droplets of oil will continue to come up for an hour or longer. These all have to be wiped off," advises T.C.

3. The teak oil takes a minimum of 2 hours for the first heavy coat to dry. When it is dry, T.C. rubs the wood with 0000 steel wool, also with the grain. Next comes a thorough cleaning of the wood with air or a tack cloth.

The procedure for the two subsequent coats follows that of the first, except that T.C. relies on 500-grit wet/dry paper to apply the second coat and 600-grit the third. "The fine sandpaper removes the *continued*

IN SEARCH OF THE PERFECT FINISH

continued

For his homemade finish, T.C. requires paper towels, 0000 steel wool, cheesecloth, cotton cloths, 400–600-grit wet/dry sandpaper, SeaFin Teak Oil, and a block of beeswax.

tiny wood-grain hairs that the oil raises," notes T.C. "The paper also 'pushes' oil into the grain and fills the pores with fine wood particles at the same time."

4. Because the oil/beeswax mixture is flammable, T.C. uses a double boiler to keep it away from the direct heat. In this arrangement, T.C. heats the teak oil to between 120–140°F (read with a candy thermometer) and adds beeswax at the rate of ¾ ounce (dry weight) to 8 ounces of oil. Frequent stirring blends the mix,

but it's the one-day curing time that really does the trick. Says T.C., "The standing time, and the subsequent reheating before use, allow the mixture to blend much better than any simple stirring I could do. It's like the taste of stew the second day—much improved with age."

5. T.C. applies his hot oil/wax solution with a soft cotton cloth. He works on only a few feet of surface at a time.

6. After T.C. covers the entire project, he goes back over the

wood cross-grain with cheesecloth pads to remove any unabsorbed mixture. To keep a fresh cloth surface working, he frequently turns the pads inside-out. A final pass goes with the grain.

T.C. repeats the whole process after the first oil/wax coat has completely dried (up to 24 hours). To complete his finish, T.C. adds two coats of a good quality paste wax, such as Minwax, and buffs.

"The final finish has a glow you can't obtain by simply putting paste wax over oil," the craftsman comments. "Although the process is lengthy, you don't need any special equipment. And, if the finish gets damaged, you can renew it easily with two coats of the oil/wax mix. Occasional buffing with a soft cloth, and a coat of paste wax once a year, is all the maintenance normally required."

Buying Guide

• **SeaFin Teak Oil.** Daly's, 3525 Stoneway No., Seattle, WA 98103. Call 206-633-4200, or 800-735-7019 for nearest dealer and for current prices.

• **Beeswax.** Available at most hardware stores.

• **Cabinetmaker's Paste Finishing Wax.** T.C. has equal results with several brands.

CHOOSING THE RIGHT CLEAR FINISH FOR YOUR PROJECT

You've swept the shop clean, waited for the glue to dry, and now your masterpiece sits there in all its wooden nakedness. The grain is beautiful. The craftsmanship top rate. So what are you going to do to it now? What type of finish will you select? How much more time do you want to spend? Read on for answers that will help you decide.

Most woodworkers would rather spend their time making sawdust than thinking about which finish to use on their projects. That's understandable, but unfortunate because the finish you apply to your creation is vitally important. A clear finish enhances the appearance of the piece as well as protects the wood against moisture, dust, and wear.

Shopping for wood finishes these days isn't easy. A surprising array of products competes for your attention and your dollar. Therefore, the more you know about clear finishes and what they'll do, the easier the selection process will become.

Factors affecting your choice

When it's time to finish your project, you can narrow your choices somewhat by asking yourself these questions:

1. How and where will the project be used? A dining room table, for example, requires a very durable finish to withstand the spills and constant wear it will encounter in use. A picture frame, on the other hand, won't need as much protection.

2. Should it have a natural-looking, low-sheen finish that accents the texture and grain of the wood, or a finish with depth that can be polished to a very high luster? Even though appearance is largely a matter of personal preference, the design itself and the type of wood used should help you make the decision.

3. How much time and effort are you willing to expend applying the finish? While some finishes are easy to work with, others require more skill and equipment to apply correctly.

Note: Until you have some experience with a finish, it's not possible to know for sure if you'll like what it does to a certain wood species. For this reason, always test the finish you select first on scrap.

The two clear-finish categories

Clear finishes today fall into one of two categories: *penetrating* finishes and *surface* (or built-up)

finishes. The penetrating ones—tung oil, linseed oil, Danish oil, mineral oil, and salad bowl finishes—soak down into the pores of the wood, forming a finish that resides in the wood itself. You wipe these on with a cloth or the palm of your hand, which makes the application practically mistake-proof.

Not surprisingly, surface finishes—natural varnish, polyurethane varnish, shellac, lacquer, and latex finishes—lie on top of the wood surface, and build up with successive coats. These either brush or spray on and usually require the use of abrasives to rub out and polish the final surface.

Types of surface finishes

Natural varnish. This product, made from natural resins (secretions), has been used by woodworkers for years. In fact, much of the furniture you see in antique shops was probably originally finished with natural varnish because of its ability to render a durable finish capable of resisting water, alcohol, and wear. Varnish is also easily brushed on and rubbed out. Because of its amber color, it gives wood a deep, rich-looking tone.

continued

CHOOSING THE RIGHT CLEAR FINISH FOR YOUR PROJECT
continued

WHEN TO USE WHICH CLEAR FINISH			
Item Type	Brand or Type Finish	Finish Category	Qualities
Toys	Watco Danish Oil	Penetrating	Nontoxic (after 30 days), durable and easily repaired, natural-looking, low sheen
	Behlen's Salad Bowl Finish	Penetrating	Durable, natural-looking, satin-sheen
	Numerous Latex Finishes	Surface	Hard, durable, good depth, dries very clear
Food-Contact Items	Behlen's Salad Bowl Finish	Penetrating	Highly resistant to moisture and food substances, natural-looking satin-sheen, easily renewed.
	Watco Danish Oil	Penetrating	Nontoxic (in 30 days), durable, easily renewed, natural-looking, low-sheen
	Mineral Oil	Penetrating	Some moisture resistance, little wear protection, easily renewed, very low-luster
Low-Use Furniture	Lacquer	Surface	Moderately durable, rich-looking, easily polished to luster
	Water-based	Surface	Good depth and durability, adds no tone
	Paste Varnish	Surface	Good durability, tones wood lightly, low build-up, hand-rubbed look, easily applied and repaired
	Tung Oil	Penetrating	Durable, moisture-resistant, nondarkening, low-luster natural appearance, easily applied/renewed
	Danish Oil	Penetrating	Durable, easily repaired, warm tone, natural-looking, slightly more sheen than tung oil
	Oil/Varnish Mix	Penetrating	Extremely durable, natural appearance, easily, more protection and sheen than oil alone

Unfortunately, natural varnishes dry very slowly (24–48 hours). Dust problems and the faster-drying synthetic varnishes have nearly eliminated natural varnishes. Except for marine and spar varnishes, which are for exterior use, you may even have a difficult time finding a supplier that carries one.

Synthetic varnish. Most varnishes today contain the newer synthetic resins and are known as polyurethane varnishes. These finishes have become quite popular with professional woodworkers and home hobbyists because they're durable, moisture-resistant, and fast-drying. They also give wood the same warm tone and depth as natural varnishes. Keep in mind, though, that these extremely hard surfaces require more effort to rub out and to polish than some of the other finishes.

Paste varnishes. Varnishes offer another option when choosing a polyurethane finish. These finishes resemble petroleum jelly in consistency and are easy to apply with a rag. They share all the advantages of polyurethane finishes, without the brush mark and settling dust problems normally associated with brushed or sprayed-on types. Because they form a thin finish with little surface buildup, poly paste varnishes create a natural-looking, low-sheen finish.

Item Type	Brand or Type Finish	Finish Category	Qualities
Hard-Use Furniture	Polyurethane Varnish	Surface	Excellent durability, high moisture and wear resistance, good depth, various lusters, lightly tones wood
	Paste Varnish	Surface	Comparable to above in durability, less surface build-up, natural-looking, easily applied/repaired
	Oil/Varnish	Penetrating	Good durability, moisture resistance, satin-luster, natural-looking, easily applied/repaired
Antiques	Oil/Varnish Mix	Penetrating:	Good durability, hand-rubbed look, natural, satin-luster, lightly tones wood, easily applied/repaired
	Paste Varnish	Surface	Hand-rubbed look with slight surface build-up, good durability, adds warm tone, easily applied and repaired
	Tung Oil	Penetrating	Durable, adds light tone, low-luster, hand-rubbed look
	Linseed Oil	Penetrating	Some durability, deepens wood tone, very low-luster, hand-rubbed look
Outdoor Projects	Spar or Marine Varnish	Surface	Exceptionally durable, highly moisture-resistant, deepens wood tone, builds depth, high-gloss
	Exterior Polyurethane	Surface	Durable and long-lasting, highly moisture-resistant, looks very similar to natural varnish
	Varathane Plastic Oil	Penetrating	Durable and long-lasting, easily renewed, satin-sheen, natural-looking

Lacquer. The fast-drying champion of finishes, lacquer is used extensively in the furniture-manufacturing industry. Though not quite as durable as varnish, lacquer does produce a moisture- and wear-resistant finish that polishes easily to a lustrous sheen. Because of the rapid drying times (approximately 30 minutes), you'll find spraying the most effective way to apply lacquer. Slower-drying, brushing lacquers make lacquer more practical for the home craftsman. Brushing lacquers still dry quickly, so restrict their use to small projects in which you can cover the entire surface in a short time.

Because lacquer is incompatible with most other finishing materials, you must use a sealer before applying lacquer to keep oil-based stains and fillers from bleeding through the finish.

Water-based. Although these finishes contain few solvents, they form a surprisingly durable and water-resistant finish when cured. The absence of noxious odors and the convenience of water cleanup make them a joy to use.

Straight from the can, these products have a milky-white appearance that transforms into a clear film when dry. Because of this clarity, they lack the rich-looking tone produced by varnish, but the finish is appropriate where minimal color change is desired. You can brush water-based finishes on easily, but they don't respond well to polishing or hand rubbing, so removing imperfections will be more difficult. Despite these short-comings, in situations where ventilation or the use of traditional solvent-based products presents a problem, water-based finishes provide you with a viable alternative.

Penetrating oil finishes
Tung oil. A centuries-old finish that's enjoying great popularity
continued

CHOOSING THE RIGHT CLEAR FINISH FOR YOUR PROJECT
continued

today, tung oil comes in two forms—pure tung oil and polymerized tung oil. Of the two, polymerized dries much faster and has more luster. Both have a light golden color that imparts just the right amount of tone to accent the grain and texture of wood surfaces. And both form a moisture-resistant, durable coating that dries to a hard, solid film.

To apply tung oil, simply wipe it on with a cloth, let it set for several minutes, then remove the excess.

Linseed oil. Even though this old-time favorite yields a finish that looks "hand-rubbed," it has some shortcomings that limit its use. In addition to its tendency to deepen the color of most woods, linseed oil never thoroughly cures, and therefore lacks durability, and darkens and deteriorates with age. Some furniture craftsmen still stand by boiled linseed oil, but with few exceptions, other penetrating oils are superior.

Danish oil. A blend of natural oils, such as tung and linseed, and small amounts of resins, Danish oils create a natural-looking finish superior to pure natural oils alone. Danish oils greatly enhance the grain pattern and texture of the wood and, at the same time, provide a durable finish that's easy to apply and maintain. Some blends, because they contain a few resins, give wood a very natural look. Others, containing more resins, impart more sheen.

Oil/varnish mixtures. For people who prefer a natural-looking, wipe-on finish with more surface protection than pure or Danish oils, a mixture of oil and varnish can be the answer. Finishes that are blends of tung oil and polyurethane are extremely durable and moisture-resistant. Apply these like penetrating oils.

Nontoxic finishes. Many wooden items that contact food or the mouth—toys, cutting boards, salad bowls, and the like—require a nontoxic finish. With penetrating finishes made specifically for these items, you simply wipe on the product and buff out the surface for a protective satin sheen that increases luster with additional applications. You can easily renew the finish when necessary.

Mineral oil, a common household item, also works as a nontoxic finish. This oil provides wood with some degree of protection, but it never really hardens.

Note: Before applying any finish, be sure to read the container's label directions carefully. Also keep in mind that many of these products are toxic, so you need to keep them out of reach of children. When applying finishes, work in a well-ventilated area that's well lit. Make sure, too, to work well away from any heat source because some of these finishes contain thinners, which can ignite easily.

MAKE THAT OLD FINISH LOOK LIKE NEW AGAIN

Stripping an old finish isn't a pleasant task, so why do it if you can avoid it? Fortunately, the right materials, some know-how, and a little ingenuity will often save that "doomed" piece you've been meaning to work on.

A good cleaning may do the trick

Dirt, oil, and wax combine and accumulate to darken and dull finishes on wood furniture. Even the rejuvenation of a lack-luster, near-antique might be as simple as cleaning with an appropriate cleanser. Murphy's Oil Soap—one commonly available, old-time favorite—cleans and conditions at the same time.

Varnish, recognizable by its tiny surface cracks, cleans well with a 50:50 mix of turpentine and tung oil (or boiled linseed oil). Rub the dirty surface with a cloth saturated in the mixture.

Some finishes will be so heavily coated with dirt and grime that you'll have to use 0000 steel wool with the cleanser. Scrub lightly with the grain to avoid scratches.

How to remove surface blemishes

All furniture picks up minor surface scratches during normal use. Moisture, too, shows up as surface cloudiness or rings left by drinking glasses. The following tips will help you cope with these problems.

Abrasions on surface-finished items. Combat tiny scratches with the help of finely ground abrasive powders. Pumice, a powdered volcanic ash, has a medium grit. Mixed to a paste with lemon oil, it polishes well. Working with the grain, rub the paste into the finish with a felt pad until the scratches disappear. Wipe off the pumice paste with a clean cloth. For a higher gloss, follow the same procedure using rottenstone, a much finer abrasive powder of ground slate.

Abrasions on oil-finished wood. On pieces finished with penetrating oil (Danish, tung, or linseed), bad spots are easy to repair. Just rub the marred area with 0000 steel wool, then apply a new coat of the appropriate oil to the entire surface.

Stubborn small scratches. Resistance to the pumice-and-rottenstone treatment calls for a heavy remedy. Step up to silicon-carbide (wet/dry) sandpaper. To use it, pour a small amount of lemon oil on the surface, then sand lightly with the grain until the blemish disappears. Start with finer grit 600 and progress down to heavier grit 320 as the blemish's stubbornness dictates.

Moisture-caused blemishes. Wet glass rings and surface cloudiness usually surrender to the pumice-and-oil-paste treatment mentioned above if the moisture hasn't penetrated too deeply. If spots resist, the only solution is sanding and refinishing.

How to camouflage deep scratches

When a scratch digs through the finish and damages the wood itself, abrasive remedies won't work. With patience and considerable practice, you could learn to fill scratches with hot lacquer sticks or cover them by spot refinishing, both permanent repairs. There are some less-permanent (and easier to accomplish) techniques, however, that will hide the damage.

• Shoe polish in a matching shade is a quick trick. Use a cotton swab or a toothpick to apply, then bring to a shine with a soft cloth.

• Defects that actually need filling are easy to conceal with putty sticks. They contain a waxy putty and come in a wide range of wood tones. Rub the tip of the stick (much like a crayon) back and forth over the scratch. Since they remain soft, don't use them on surfaces such as tabletops and chair arms.

• Scratches on hard-use surfaces should be stained to match, then filled with spot-finishing lacquer on an artist's brush. Polish the filled scratch with pumice and rottenstone.

Caring for fine wood furniture

Once the finish is refurbished, light maintenance keeps it in shape.

Avoid wax buildup. Dust furniture weekly with lemon oil sprinkled on a soft cloth.

Polish only when necessary. Spray-on and liquid polishes should be applied only when furniture actually needs polishing, not for weekly dusting.

Use paste wax only twice a year. Paste wax provides long-lasting sheen and a thicker protective barrier than spray-on and liquid polishes, but builds up fast. Therefore, apply it only every six months. When you note a paste-wax-polished wood finish getting tacky to the touch, dull, and attracting fingerprints, don't put on more; there's too much already. Clean off the buildup with the oil soap or 50:50 mix of tung oil and turpentine mentioned earlier.

FIVE EASY STEPS TO A GLASS-SMOOTH FINISH

One morning not long ago, Design Editor Jim Downing marched into the *WOOD*® magazine shop carrying a smooth-as-glass tabletop that he had made for the galley of his 30' sailboat. Not surprisingly, it brought on a chorus of "oohs" and "aahs" as staffers rushed to run their fingers across it. Right away we knew that Jim's polyurethane-finish technique was too good to keep a secret from our faithful readers.

The key supplies for Jim's glass-smooth finish include 1,500-grit sandpaper and two finishing compounds formulated for auto finishes. In case you can't find a local auto-supply dealer that carries these products, we've arranged for a mail-order source. And, you won't need any special tools—just some patience and a little elbow grease.

1. For starters, sand the wood surface smooth with 150-grit paper. If you plan to stain the piece, sand it again with 220-grit

paper. If you used an orbital sander, be sure to closely inspect the surface under sidelighting and sand away any swirly marks.

Now, carefully remove the sawdust from the surface with compressed air. Otherwise, vacuum the surface and clean it with a tack rag. If you prefer a stained surface, apply an oil-based stain and allow it to dry for 24 hours.

2. Coat the end grain of the surface with polyurethane, and allow it to saturate the pores fully before applying any finish to the tabletop. After a couple of minutes, and 2–4 applications, the end grain will stop absorbing polyurethane. Now, coat the top by brushing the polyurethane *across* the grain as

shown *below left,* then brush *with* the grain to completely fill the wood pores. If you stained the piece, allow this coat to dry completely before proceeding.

For unstained wood, immediately wipe away the excess polyurethane with a 6–8" squeegee as shown *below.* The squeegee helps drive the material down into the wood pores, and leaves almost no finish on the high grain.

After the first coat of poly-urethane dries (on either the stained or unstained piece), lightly smooth the surface with 150–grit sandpaper, being careful not to sand through the finish of the stained piece. With a fast-drying polyurethane you can apply your

second coat after 12 hours. For slower-drying polyurethanes, wait 24 hours between coats.

Apply and squeegee a second coat to the stained or unstained piece. After this coat dries, inspect the surface in a strong sidelight to see if the grain has filled to your satisfaction. If not, sand with 150-grit paper and repeat the process. Sand the final coat with 150- and 220-grit papers. For the porous red oak end table in this story, we applied and squeegeed four coats to completely fill the grain.

3. Next, spray a heavy, flowing coat of polyurethane onto the surface. Apply three more coats, and sand between them with 220-grit paper. (Aerosol cans work fine if you don't own a spray gun.) After the final coat dries, apply a few ounces of water and wet-sand the surface with a 3M

No. 20 wet or dry sponge pad and 1,500-grit paper as shown *below left*. Check for glossy spots and resand any missed areas. You can purchase the pad, 1,500-grit paper, and finishing compounds through the Buying Guide at *right*.

4. Build that glowing finish with 3M's Finesse-it II Finishing Material. Squirt an ounce or two of the liquid onto the surface and rub it in with a clean, soft rag as shown *below right*. Bear down hard as you rub the entire surface. Then, wipe the surface clean, and if you see any dull areas that you missed, redo them.

5. For the final luster, repeat Step 4 with 3M's Imperial Hand Glaze. Be careful to use separate, clean rags for steps 4 and 5.

From beginning to end, we spent five days finishing the end table's oak surface. Less-porous woods, such as cherry, maple, or walnut, require about half that much time.

Buying Guide
• **3M Finesse-it II Finishing Material and Imperial Hand Glaze,** 1,500-grit sandpaper, and No. 20 wet or dry sponge pad. Available at Auto-paint supply stores, or contact Hawkeye Auto Supply, 417 12th St., Des Moines, IA 50309.

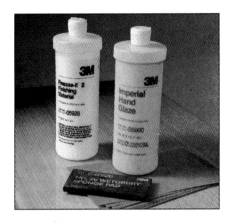

LACQUER MAY BE PERFECT FOR YOU

Lacquer has long been the mainstay finish of the furniture manufacturer and professional finisher. Its ability to produce a pleasing yet subdued luster finish rivals any finish alternative. Lacquer can, and will, give your work that professional touch, too—if you carry out the essential steps with care.

Finishes that stand out beg to be looked at and to be touched. We all appreciate and would like to be able to produce these ultrafine finishes ourselves. Fortunately, these pride-builders really aren't all that difficult to work with. And lacquer, once you know and understand how to use it, can be your new finish standard. We consulted with our project builder Jim Boelling. Lacquer happens to be Jim's absolute favorite finish. He's been using it on his projects for about 20 years.

Just what is lacquer, anyway?

If you take a look at the contents on a can of lacquer, you'll see nitrocellulose, the same stuff they use in gunpowder, making up the solid phase of the formula. It forms the actual film you put on the wood.

There's another detail you'll note reading the contents label. Lacquer contains only 20–30 percent solids. When you thin it for application, you reduce the solids content still more. As a result, you really don't apply very much material in one coating. By comparison, varnish typically contains about 50 percent solids.

The other ingredients in lacquer, with their long scientific names, simply dissolve and carry the nitrocellulose. They evaporate quickly after application.

The advantages warrant considering lacquer

Longtime lacquer advocates, such as Jim Boelling, prefer lacquer as an indoor finish because it produces a flexible but tough film that resists wear and normal use. It's easy to apply, and dries fast, too.

Because of the low solids content, each lacquer application puts down a very thin film. To create a high-quality finish, you have to apply multiple coats to build up the film. Fortunately, each new coat melts into the lacquer, making one tight-bonding film. You simply sand lightly between coats.

Lacquer has another advantage, too—it's easy to sand, rub, and polish the film to get the degree of luster you desire.

Two, four, or how many more spray coats?

"If you're after a quality lacquer finish," Jim Boelling says, "forget the shortcuts. For a good finish, you have to apply numerous coats, and that takes time and effort. If you don't have the time to work lacquer the way it should be worked, you'll probably be better off using some other finishing product."

So, how many coats do you need to apply? Our answer may sound evasive to you, but really it isn't. The number of coats depends on just how good a finish you want and what you are working with.

Lacquer has a selfish quirk—it only works with certain products. For example, using lacquer over oil- or varnish-based fillers or sealers can be touchy. The strong solvents in the lacquer can soften, dissolve, or even "lift" incompatible underlying materials and cause bleeding and adhesion problems. You can try to seal them with just a light mist coat of lacquer sealer. But

to be safe, Boelling recommends using only materials formulated for lacquers.

It's best to spray lacquer, but you can brush it, too

Spraying produces the smoothest surface, free of brush marks and contaminants. On woods that give off color, or if you want to lacquer over a filler or stain, spraying may be the only way to avoid lifting or smearing them.

You can also buy lacquer in aerosol cans. We find they serve nicely around the *WOOD®* shop for touch-up and many small jobs. "But," warns Boelling, "aerosol lacquer comes highly thinned, so you'll need to apply even more coats to get the desired film depth."

If you want to brush on lacquer, and that makes sense on small projects, buy a *brush formulation*. Brush types dry slower than sprays, so you have more time to apply.

Directions call for thinning lacquer sealer and the gloss coats. But be sure to use thinners compatible with the lacquer you buy. If you don't know which one to buy, check the can's label.

If you spray during hot, humid weather, consider adding a blushing agent to the mixture. It helps keep the lacquer from turning white (milking). This problem occurs when the nitrocellulose absorbs moisture from the atmosphere and traps it in the finish.

Build film with gloss coats

The real advantage of lacquer lies in the ease with which you can *control* the exact surface sheen wanted. Typically, you start by applying two or more thin coats of lacquer sealer.

Sanding between sealer coats (and all coats) removes surface blemishes and levels the surface.

Sanding sealer films can be built up, but Boelling advises not to let them. Sand off most of the sealer.

To build up the film, use gloss lacquer—it produces a tough, clear film. If you want a high gloss as the final surface, use it for the topcoat, too. Then rub and polish as little or as much as you need to get the luster you want.

Earlier we said there were no shortcuts. Well, there's one. Apply a satin- or semigloss-formulated lacquer for the final coat. Or, add a flattening agent to the gloss lacquer. Both produce a lower surface sheen.

You can use a number of materials to produce the final finish. We've heard of woodworkers using everything from steel wool and beeswax to rubbing with pumice and paraffin oil. A few even swear by the special automobile rubbing compounds and pastes they've uncovered along the way.

Proper application: The key to a quality finish

Equipment you need: Use an air compressor or an airless spray system. Compressors with an air tank and capable of supplying at least 50 pounds of pressure work best. Select a siphon-feed gun with an external mix nozzle and a needle sized for lacquer.

Adjustments to make: Set the pressure regulator to provide good spray atomization—between 35 and 50 psi—but without causing misting. Fan-shaped patterns work best for spraying flat, wide surfaces; use a round pattern for small, irregular surfaces or close work. To make the pattern you want, test-spray on paper or cardboard. Adjust the *pattern control* (top control knob on a gun) holding the gun 6"–10" from the spray surface. Adjust the *fluid control* knob until the gun applies the amount of spray you want. If the spray looks too fine or light, *reducing* air pressure or *opening* the fluid control *increases* droplet size and flow rate. If the spray appears too coarse, *closing* the fluid control *reduces* both flow rate and droplet size.

Holding the gun: Hold the gun at a uniform distance from the spray surface. Avoid arcing your spray strokes—arcing causes more spray to be deposited at the center than at the ends. Move the gun across the surface at a constant speed that's comfortable for you. Pull the trigger as you reach the leading edge, and release the trigger as you reach the opposite edge. Tip: Making a single full stroke parallel to the ends of the piece ensures complete coverage and eliminates waste trying to spray to the very edges.

Best spraying sequence: Make the top or outside edge of the previous stroke your aiming point so each pass overlaps the other by 50 percent. This provides double coverage and a wet coat without streaking. If you want to double-coat, apply the first coat, stroking *with* the grain. Spray the second coat *across* the grain.

Spray *outside* corners straight-on to coat the edges uniformly. On slender items, such as table legs, adjust the gun's pattern to fit the surface to reduce overspray. On *inside* corners, spray each side of the corner, only slightly overlapping. Overlap 50 percent on round objects.

continued

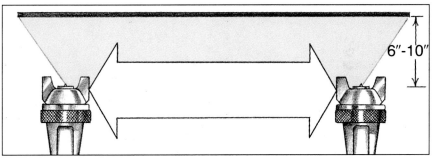

6"-10"

Move gun at constant speed and maintain uniform gun-to-surface distance to deposit an even coat.

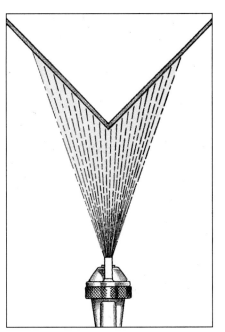

Spray outside corners straight-on.

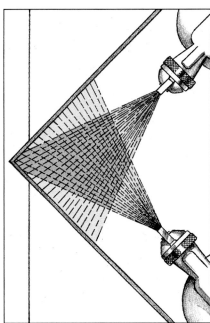

Spray each side of an inside corner separately with small overlap.

LACQUER MAY BE PERFECT FOR YOU
continued

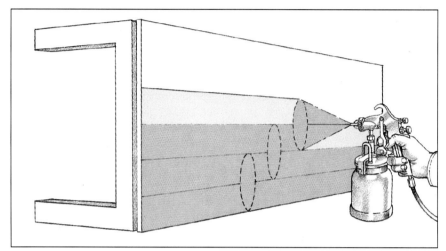

Overlap previous spray lap 50 percent for uniform wet coat. Let overspray fall on unsprayed area.

INCORRECT

CORRECT

On long surfaces, brush lengthwise full length of surface rather than in short lengths.

The proper brushing technique: Select a medium-soft, natural-bristle brush. (You can use a small foam brush or nylon wipes for small jobs.) Load the brush to about one-half the depth of the bristles, then wipe excess from the tip on the edge of the can. Flow the lacquer onto the surface, working with the grain, and from dry to wet surfaces. Reload the brush frequently and don't spread the lacquer too much. Work in strips about 1½ times the brush's width. To avoid obvious brushing patterns,

work lengthwise with the surface rather than in short lengths across it. Avoid overlapping onto a partially set area—you can coat missed areas later. Brush out any air bubbles.

Eight steps to a perfect lacquer finish

Note: Follow a planned program to ensure best results. With experience, you will probably develop your own step-by-step system. In the meantime, here's an outline to get you started:

Play it safe

Be aware of two major inherent hazards—the possibility of explosion, and the chance of bodily injury from direct contact.

The chief culprits: the solvents and thinners in lacquer. When volatilized or atomized into fine droplets in the air, they form mixtures that can ignite by an open flame or spark. If you smoke, or if you have to do the spraying in a confined area where there are pilot lights or other kinds of ignitors, use a different finishing product.

Confine spraying area

Apply lacquer only in areas with adequate ventilation. If you must spray indoors, confine it to a properly designed and equipped booth. Mechanical exhaust fans provide the most positive ventilation. However, the ventilator motors must be *flame-* or *spark-proof*, too. As a further precaution, use only explosion-proof lights in the spray area.

If you can't spray at home, try to rent time in a professional spray booth at a business or school. Or hire a shop to do it.

Protect your body, too

Minimize direct physical contact with lacquer and thinners. Wear protective gloves to cover your hands, goggles to protect your eyes, and a chemical-filtering respirator to protect your air passages and lungs. Your dealer should be able to supply you with the necessary protective equipment, or direct you to a source.

Do not rely on lightweight paper dust masks. They won't adequately protect you against noxious vapors and the fine spray mists.

1. Prepare the wood. First, check joints for traces of glue. Wetting the wood around glue joints with lacquer thinner shows up embedded glue. Sand off any trace of glue.

Sand to level the wood surface. Start sanding with a coarse grade of sandpaper—80- or 100-grit—and mount it on a wood or rubber block. Sand with the grain. Use progressively finer grit sandpapers to remove sanding marks.

2. Inspect the wood. Rotate the piece in front of a bright light and inspect it from a variety of angles (photo A). Look for shadows that show up dents, scratches, and other surface marks.

Sand any flaws you find.

As you sand, inspect the wood surface with strong cross light to spot dents and scratches that need to be sanded before lacquering.

3. Stain the project. Stain or fill the wood with lacquer-compatible products only, if desired.

4. Prepare the lacquer sealer. To thin for spraying, test with a viscosimeter (photo B). Compare that time with the value suggested for lacquer on the viscosimeter. If it takes longer, add more thinner.

Mix the lacquer sealer and thinner with a clean paddle—do not shake. Warm the lacquer by placing it in a pan of hot (140 degrees F.) tap water. Heating drives out air bubbles and helps the lacquer flow on the surface better. If brushing, follow thinning directions on the can.

5. Apply the sealer. Spray on a thin, even coat, until the entire surface appears wet. Let the sealer dry for an hour or two, then sand smooth with 320-grit sandpaper. Sand in one direction. Back the sandpaper with a firm rubber or felt pad. Sanding produces a white dusting on the wood surface (photo C). Sand away most of the lacquer sealer, but do not sand through to bare wood. Apply a second coat of sealer, let dry, then sand.

If brush-applying, apply a thin coat, as uniformly as possible.

Test viscosity by timing flow rate through a viscosimeter. You can buy one at a paint store.

6. Inspect the sealer. Remove the sanding dust and look for shiny spots or areas. If you see both dull and shiny spots, it means the surface has not been completely leveled and you need to apply another coat of sealer. The mottled appearance of the clothes hanger (photo D), indicates it needs another coat.

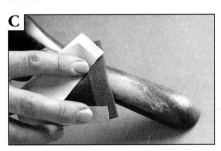

Sand the sealer to level the surface. Back sandpaper with a firm block for sanding on flat surfaces, a foam pad for irregular surfaces.

7. Build up lacquer coats. Use gloss lacquer for the buildup coats. Use a viscosimeter to determine how much you need to thin, or thin about 25 percent. Warm the lacquer in a hot-tap-water bath.

Apply a uniform coat, just heavy enough to wet the surface. If brushing, apply enough so the lacquer flows and levels itself.

Let the lacquer dry for an hour or two, then sand lightly with 320-grit sandpaper. Sand to level surface and correct imperfections.

If pores are visible in the film surface, it needs more buildup and leveling. You want to see a perfectly level surface without any pores.

Apply the top or finish coat full strength (undiluted). For a high-gloss finish, use gloss lacquer for the final coat. Allow it to dry several days before rubbing.

Glossy areas show low spots. Apply more sealer coats to fill low spots and sand the surface.

8. Rub out the topcoat. Dip a felt pad in a mixture of pumice rubbing compound and paraffin oil, and rub lacquered surface (photo E).

You want a uniform luster, so as the final step, polish with rotten-stone and paraffin oil, a rubbing compound, or a special nylon rubbing pad. Finally, apply a wax or lemon oil, and then polish.

Use a felt pad such as a felt eraser, and rub, first with a mixture of pumice and paraffin oil, then with rottenstone and oil.

FERN WEBER'S LACQUER FINISH

Carving competition judges don't give out ribbons for the best finish on a carving, but if they did, you can bet your bottom dollar that Fern Weber would win her share of blues. In fact, we think it's partly her expertise at finishing that helped her and her husband, Walt, walk off with the Best Overall Display Award at the 1987 Kansas City-Area Woodcarvers' Show. Of course, having top-quality carvings beneath that finish didn't hurt the Missouri couple, either. We asked Fern how on earth she gives her projects such a heavenly look. Now that she's told us, we're passing along the good finishing news to you.

When Fern enrolled in a tole-painting class a decade ago, she never dreamed of getting involved in carving, or finishing for that matter. About the same time, Fern convinced her soon-to-be retired husband to sign up for a wood-carving class to keep him busy. To her surprise and delight, Walt really took to carving—and became very good.

The only thing is, it seems Walt liked to carve a lot more than he liked applying the finish to his projects. That's when Fern offered her help, and ever since then she's been "tidying up" and finishing Walt's—and now her own—carvings.

Fern says that it was her tole painting instructor who impressed on her the importance of properly preparing a project for finishing. "She was very, very particular," says Fern, "and I've always been a thorough person, too—a characteristic I picked up over the years from my mother."

While obviously it helps to be meticulous in approach, Fern gives part of the credit for her success to a set of riffler files she uses to smooth the surface after the carving is complete. "They're the greatest thing I've ever found to smooth projects. They come in all sorts of shapes—I've got a couple dozen of them, I suppose. They're a must for anyone who wants to do good-quality work."

But there's more to this amazingly smooth finish than careful preparation of the surface. As any good wood finisher, Fern has definite preferences when it comes to the products she applies to her carvings. After a lot of trial and error over the years, she's settled on—and swears by—McCloskey's Stain Controller and Wood Sealer, Deft Semi-Gloss Clear Wood Finish (a brushing lacquer), and Butcher's Boston Polish Paste Wax. (See the Buying Guide on *page 46* for information on where to purchase these products, as well as the riffler files Fern uses for smoothing wood surfaces.)

How good is Fern Weber's brushed lacquer finish, really? She and Walt sell many of their carvings over the counter at mall exhibitions, crafts fairs, and the like, and she says, "We always encourage people to pick up our projects and feel them. That's what usually closes the sale." One recent

Padauk dolphins carved by Walt Weber and finished by Fern

Cypress-knee carving titled "Meditation"

1

2

3

4

customer said, according to Fern, that "once you feel the finish on one of Fern's carvings, you've just got to have more." That same customer has just placed an order for another $450 worth of Fern's carefully crafted carvings.

Here's how Fern finishes her projects—step-by-step

1. Because Fern executes sleek and stylized carvings, they just have to be smooth. She removes any evidence of knife cuts and gets into all those grooves and hard-to-get-at places with her set of riffler files. "They make very fine cuts," Fern says, "so smooth in fact that I almost never need to use coated abrasives coarser than 220-grit."

2. When she deems the piece ready for sanding, Fern exchanges the riffler files for sandpaper. "I try to sand with the grain whenever possible, and I gauge the final readiness by feeling the project rather than looking at it. You can feel when its ready; don't hurry," she says. Note the "remodeled" Rubbermaid Spice Carousel that Fern uses to store her carving tools.

Walt bored holes in the carousel so the tools stand upright.

3. With her carefully prepared project in hand, Fern applies one coat of McCloskey's sealer with an inexpensive nylon brush. "I wipe off the excess sealer with a clean, lint-free rag and let the sealer dry for 24 hours," Fern notes. "That drying time is important; the following coat of Deft will bubble if you put it on before the sealer has dried completely," she adds. "In fact, the label on the sealer says not to use McCloskey's under a lacquer finish, but it works well for me."

continued

FERN WEBER'S LACQUER FINISH
continued

Fern buys this product in quart containers, then divides the contents into several small jars with tight-fitting lids. Doing this, she says, prevents the sealer in the unused jars from congealing.

4. When applying the Deft Semi-Gloss Clear Wood Finish—sometimes up to ten coats—Fern takes great pains to brush the lacquer in one direction only. And she insists on a camel's hair lacquer brush. "Less-expensive brushes just don't lay down the finish as smoothly as the camel's hair," Fern advises.

"I like to wait at least an hour between coats, and don't forget to steel-wool and tack-cloth your project between coats," she says.

5. After each coat of Deft, Fern sands all surfaces, including the cracks and grooves with 0000 (the finest) steel wool. "Doing this," she says, "removes the hairlike grain the Deft finish raises. The softer the wood, the more severe the grainraising." A careful wiping of the surface with a tack cloth removes all metal shards left as the result of sanding.

6. "After the final coat and a light rubbing with steel wool, I apply three coats of the Butcher's Wax," Fern counsels. "I leave each coat of wax on for about 20 minutes before buffing it with a clean cloth. Old diapers work well here."

Buying Guide
• **Rifflers (files).** Several sets available from Woodcraft, 210 Wood County Industrial Park, P.O. Box 1686, Parkersburg, WV 26102-1686. Call 800-535-4482 for a catalog.
• **McCloskey Stain Controller and Wood Sealer (Clear).** The McCloskey Corp., Philadelphia, PA. Call 800-345-4530 for the name of the nearest distributor.
• **Deft Semi-Gloss Clear Wood Finish.** Available at many hardware and home center stores.
• **Butcher's Boston Polish Paste Wax (Amber).** Call 800-225-9475 for the name of the nearest distributor.

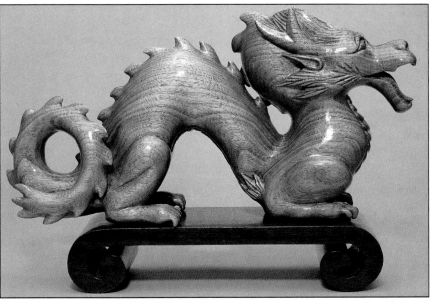

Medieval dragon carved and finished by Fern

SAL MARINO'S PERFECT FINISH

This Brooklyn-based woodworking expert puts a new spin on a classical finishing technique—French polishing. Here, he tells you how to get exactly the same high-gloss look on your turnings in a fraction of the time that it took the old masters.

The French polishing commonly found on European classical furniture produces a glasslike surface. But the process takes a long time to learn and apply.

Brooklyn craftsman Sal Marino briefly explains: "The old way, French polishing was done with shellac, alcohol, pumice powder, and elbow grease. The whole idea was to build up a very beautiful shiny finish by rubbing on coats of alcohol-thinned shellac with a pad made of wool and linen.

"A finisher continually moved the pad soaked in alcohol and shellac and peppered with pumice across the piece, pushing down as he went, " Sal goes on. "The alcohol blew off [evaporated] very quickly, leaving a thin film of shellac and pumice down in the pores. Then, he would change the proportion—increasing the shellac—as the finish built. It's quite an art."

According to Sal, modern padding lacquers, which blend shellac and lacquer with solvents and retarders, have replaced French polishing because they're easier to work with. And his *friction-film* finish for woodturnings is no exception to this advancement.

"It's very similar to French polishing as practiced by the masters because you apply pressure to the spinning piece," Sal says. "But it results in a beautiful, high-gloss, dust-free finish—just like French polishing—in a fraction of the time it would otherwise take."

Although Sal sands with six progressively finer grits of abrasives, including 1200, each sanding step only requires about 30 seconds.

Heat, the essence of a friction-film finish

How can even an inexperienced woodworker achieve such results when it takes months to perfect real French polishing? "Two reasons," Sal explains. "First, with this finish, the film actually builds up on the surface. And second, the film isn't achieved conventionally, like by spraying, but by pressure application with a cloth. As you increase the application pressure, it generates heat that dries the surface film. And as the film dries, the pressure burnishes it—as in French polishing—to make the surface really pop. That's also why it works best on turned objects— the finish requires the heat from the friction of pressure on the spinning object."

How to work up to a faux French polish

Sal admits that one of the secrets to a high-gloss, friction finish lies in the surface preparation. "If you get a real good surface from the [lathe] tool, then you don't have to do much sanding," he says.

Actually, the sanding Sal does takes little more than a few minutes because he works on a spinning vessel mounted in the lathe. Here's how he starts out:

"What I do is sand with progressively finer papers—120, 220, 320, 400, 600, then jump to 1200. They're all dry abrasive, and applied at the same speed the piece was finish-turned at," says Sal. "The 120- and 220-grit are cloth-backed garnet papers so they don't heat up my hand. When I get to the 320-grit *continued*

SAL MARINO'S PERFECT FINISH
continued

and above, I use a wet/dry paper, but without wetting it."

But how does Sal know when to switch to a finer grit? "I have a lamp mounted above the lathe that shines down on the work at a slight angle," he explains. "So, after I sand—and that's mostly done with the 120-grit to establish the scratch pattern—I wipe off the dust. Then I look at it under the light. As the piece spins, the light reveals any deeper scratches—they show up as little shadows. I sand until it has no shadows and the surface looks uniform [see photo, *page 47*], then I move on to the next higher grit."

Sal explains why he does all that sanding: "Because it's impossible to sand with the grain on a spinning piece, you get scratches. But I develop a scratch pattern that's almost invisible."

Finishing under pressure

After sanding, Sal wipes down the still-spinning piece with a cloth dampened in acetone or naphtha.

"That's important with some of the oily, exotic woods," he notes.

Now, Sal's ready to apply Woodturner's Finish (manufactured by Behlen, see Buying Guide *right*). "Woodturners Finish is a modern padding lacquer formulated specifically for the lathe," he says. "And I first apply it liberally to the piece with a pad of fine, 100-percent cotton cheesecloth, [or all-cotton T-shirt] while it spins at about 600 rpm—that's not fast enough for the finish to set up too quickly."

Next, Sal begins his polishing. "I keep the cloth moving across the piece [as shown *below*] until I begin to feel that most of the finish has been laid down—the surface starts to feel tacky," he advises. "Then, I start applying a little pressure with the pad. After about 30 seconds, the finish brightens right up. A few more passes with the cloth and that's it. If the gloss seems too high, knock it back with super-fine steel wool after it cures."

Buying Guide
• **Woodturner's Finish by Behlen.** Call Behlen at 518-843-1380 for the dealer nearest you, or order direct from Garret Wade at 800-221-2942.

Burnishing a finish gives you a deep rich gloss, as on these egg cups of zebrawood and cordia.

Light pressure on the turning wood with the pad quickly dries the finish and burnishes it. This modern version of a French polish takes but a few minutes.

POLYMERIZED TUNG OIL

Ever had the feeling that other woodworkers know a thing or two about finishing their projects that you don't? We certainly have! Some projects simply "radiate" quality, and more often than not, it's the finish that attracts your attention.

Bill Lovelace, a woodworker from Phoenix, Arizona, shared some of his finishing wisdom with us, and we think you'll agree with us that the results shown above speak for themselves. Bill finishes his Southwest-inspired stack-laminated bowls with lacquer-type sanding sealer and polymerized tung oil, and he swears that if he can get good results, the rest of us can, too. Here's how he goes about it.

Note: Not all tung oils have been polymerized. This heating process combines tung oil with selected other ingredients to create

a controlled, faster dry rate. This produces a harder, more durable, and more chemically resistant finish than nonpolymerized tung oil.

Bring on the abrasives

Bill sells a lot of his bowls, some for as much as $750. And he knows that people willing to plunk down that kind of money for a decorative bowl know the difference between quality workmanship and an inferior product. That's why he spends an hour or more sanding his bowls after turning the project.

While he could do all of the sanding by hand, Bill prefers to speed the process along by running the lathe at medium speed and

chucking up a series of flap sanders—coarse, medium, and fine—in a ⅜" reversible drill to sand both the outside and inside of the bowl (see photo A). And to smooth the bottom, he changes to a flexible sanding disc, again using several grits of abrasive (photo B).

For best results, Bill advises that you blow off the dust created by one grit before moving on to the next one. Otherwise, he says, "you end up simply moving the same dust around rather than removing more material."

Lots of woodworkers would be satisfied with the results they'd achieve with the flap sander and sanding disc, but not Bill. He also
continued

POLYMERIZED TUNG OIL
continued

sands all surfaces by hand with a succession of B-weight garnet abrasives (120-, 150-, 180-, and 220-grit).

Sanding sealer—the great time-saver

Once satisfied that the surface is ready, Bill pops the lid off one of his favorite finishing products, Parks Lacquer-Type Sanding Sealer. Like most woodworkers who have found success with a product, Bill swears by this sealer. "I apply one *thin* coat with the grain with a disposable brush, and I'm always on the lookout for drips; they take lots of elbow grease to remove." (Photo C shows how he applies it.)

Bill doesn't know specifically what's in the product that makes it dry so quickly (usually 30 minutes or less), but he appreciates that characteristic.

After allowing the sealer to dry to the touch, Bill then turns on the lathe (at medium speed) and sands all surfaces with 0000 steel wool (as shown in Photo D). He prefers steel wool over coated abrasives because he feels he has better control with it. Bill advises to apply a good amount of pressure, but "be careful when working around corners. It's easy to sand too deeply."

How does this craftsman know when the bowl is ready for the tung

oil? "I depend a lot on feel, and also visually check the surface with the bright light. The light makes spotting rough areas pretty easy."

Polymerized tung oil—the finishing touch

The second part of Bill Lovelace's one-two finishing punch is a product called Jasco Polymerized Tung Oil. (See the Buying Guide for more information on this and the sanding sealer.) Here again, he could go on the road as a promotion man for this product, claiming, "I've tried several other brands of tung oil, but I like Jasco the best."

What's his secret to success with this product? "Don't follow the directions too closely. Don't rub it in; just lay it on and leave it alone." Rotating the bowl by hand, he applies a *thin* coat of tung oil with an absorbent towel or a lint-free cloth and tries to avoid overlapping the finish (see photo E).

Twenty-four hours after applying the first coat of tung oil, Bill sands all surfaces with 0000 steel wool. "I usually put on four or five thin coats and steel-wool between each. But after the final coat, I don't do anything except allow the finish to dry. It self-levels and dries to a deep luster."

More tips from Bill on using polymerized tung oil

• Make sure the temperature is at least 70 degrees when applying the finish. Lower temperatures slow drying time and make application more difficult. They also may cause the finish to fog.

• Dust can play havoc with this finish because of its lengthy drying time. So make sure, especially on the last coat, that there's not any airborne dust floating around in the shop.

• This same finish also works well on all kinds of projects. "I just finished a grandfather clock with this tung oil, and it turned out beautifully," says Bill.

• If the project loses some of its luster after a time, you can restore the shine with lemon oil.

• To fix mistakes, sand the area with 120-grit abrasive, then apply more sanding sealer and tung oil.

Buying Guide

• **Parks Lacquer-Type Sanding Sealer.** Available in quart containers through Ace Hardware and Sherwin-Williams stores. They may have to order it.

• **Jasco Polymerized Tung Oil.** Contact Jasco at 415-968-6005 for availability in your area. Available in pints, quarts, and gallons.

THE EVER-CLEAR, NEVER-FEAR FINISH

Water-based lacquer is the answer to everything—your health, safety, the environment, and a real smooth piano-like finish that looks 30 coats deep," says Bill Aitchison of Bedford Park, Illinois.

After 30 years of painting and furniture finishing, Bill Aitchison, 50, could see the writing on the wall. His mind spun and his body reeled following every bout in the spray booth with traditional, petroleum-based, nitrocellulose lacquer. "My body was really telling me something," the Bedford Park, Illinois, craftsman recalls. "I got sick of being sick. I didn't need OSHA [Occupational Safety and Health Administration] to warn me."

He also could see the day when state and federal legislation would lower the boom on time-proven finishing methods—ones learned from his father. "I knew laws were coming down the road, like what California has done to limit emissions in the finishing industry. I had to change or quit." (See editor's note, *next page*.)

Today, even though he's spraying more than ever, Bill doesn't feel dizzy or nauseous, and no pungent odor pervades his workspace. In fact, he even recirculates the air vented from the booth through the shop to reduce his heating bill—without fearing explosion and fire. His finish: a water-based lacquer.

Clear quality to count on

"I started using Amity Clear Gloss after reading about it in a trade magazine. The article said it not only was safe because it was water-based, but also nonyellowing," Bill explains. "Somewhat suspicious, I took a two-hour drive to the company's headquarters to find out more. After a demonstration, I decided that it seemed to work."

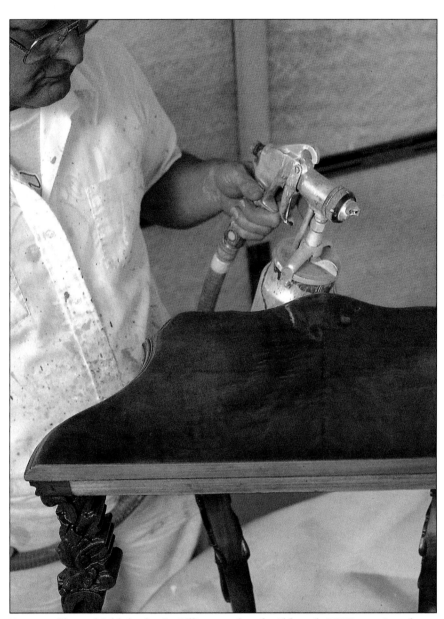

Furnace filters shield the fan in Bill's spray booth. Although OSHA requires that a mask be worn, and the manufacturer recommends it, Bill sometimes leaves it behind because water-based lacquer isn't toxic and has little overspray.

Back in his shop, Bill put his newly discovered product to the test. "I took pieces of walnut, oak, and maple, and cut them in half," he remembers. "Next, I put them on the spray table and made one pass with the nitrocellulose. Then,

I let them dry, sanded them, and put down a finish coat."

Bill duplicated the treatment using the water-based lacquer, and was dumbfounded by the outcome. "The water-based gloss had twice
continued

51

THE EVER-CLEAR, NEVER-FEAR FINISH
continued

as much build. The company claimed that it would, but I had to find out for myself." (An Amity spokesman told us that their water-based lacquer contains 30–40 percent solids, compared to 15 percent in nitrocellulose lacquer.)

And clarity? Bill has found water-based lacquer to be so clear that he has to account for it in staining. "People expect wood furniture to have a yellowish cast. To get that look with water-base, I have to add yellow to the stains," Bill notes.

In addition to its nonyellowing nature, Bill's favorite finish has proved tough and durable, too. "I've been spraying it for two years now, and not one customer has brought back a piece because the finish didn't hold up," he says. "And I mean tabletops that take abuse with meals and homework."

Mastering a new approach

Once he trusted the water-based lacquer, Bill embraced the system. Although he could have stuck with his conventional compressor to spray the new finish, he spent about $700 for a low-pressure turbine spraying system—one that utilizes an airflow of 90 cfm to atomize the finish rather than compressed air—to take the greatest advantage of the product's high-solid content and keep overspray to a minimum (see Buying Guide at the end of the article). An airflow sprayer lays down 80 percent of the finishing material. A traditional compressor nets about 40 percent.

He built an 8x10' spray booth, too, with the efficient but noisy sprayer turbine outside. For ventilation, he added a chimneylike flue fitted with an ordinary window fan and shielded by inexpensive furnace filters. The filters capture the few solids left in the air and keep them off the fan.

Air pressure affects the spraying of water-based lacquer, so Bill must occasionally check the material's viscosity by seeing how fast it flows.

Before spraying either the water-based sanding sealer ("That gives the gloss something to bite into") or the gloss, Bill measures how the material flows. "Atmospheric pressure affects its flow," says Bill, "so you have to check the material's viscosity [thickness or thinness]."

Bill determines viscosity by pouring a small amount of the material into a flow-out cup. With a stopwatch, he measures how fast it empties. "If the cup empties in under 18 seconds, it's fine," Bill advises. "If it takes longer, then I have to thin it with water."

Atmospheric pressure affects water-based lacquer by making it flow slower, but humidity has no effect because the lacquer's a water-born material. "In high humidity, nitrocellulose lacquer traps moisture, causing what's called blush," Bill says. "You have to add blush retarder to slow drying and allow the moisture to escape. Humidity doesn't bother water-based. In fact, it seems to perform better."

All set to go, Bill switches on the ventilating fan and begins laying down lacquer. "I usually put on three or four coats," he notes, "but that doesn't mean laying down a coat and letting it dry, then spraying another coat. With this stuff, you spray on wet coats. I make a pass, then do it again, then do it again. And, if I have a big run or something, I just take a sponge and water and wash it off. That is, if I repair it within two minutes, because it sets up in three minutes, hardens in an hour, and takes four days to cure."

Cleanup may be the part of spraying that irks craftsmen the most. Yet, to Bill, it's a snap. "I just walk over to the deep sink and rinse the gun out with warm water. Then, every month or two, I'll take the nozzle apart and soak it in regular lacquer thinner to cut the buildup. But it couldn't be easier."

Editor's Note: *In some California metropolitan air districts, Rule 1136 limits the amount of air-pollutants released by finishing products by lowering their volatile organic compound (VOC) content to 2.33 pounds per gallon. A gallon of nitrocellulose lacquer contains from 5 to 7 pounds while a water-based lacquer such as that used by Bill has only 2.1 pounds. Similar limits have been set in other cities and states.*

THE TRADITIONAL AMANA FINISH

Over the years, furniture made in the Amana Colonies earned a reputation for quality and fine craftsmanship. A part of that good name undoubtedly comes from its durable, yet beautiful finish. That craftsmanship tradition, started during the colonies' early days over a century ago, continues to this day.

What goes into an Amana Colonies finish? We've been curious for some time, so recently we paid a visit to the Schanz Furniture and Gift Shop at South Amana, Iowa. This gave us a great opportunity to talk about furniture finishing with owner Norman Schanz, and observe his finishing crew as they applied the "Schanz" version of the prized finish to some popular Amana offerings made in his shop.

Although techniques and products have changed over the years, Norman proudly emphasizes that he still uses many of the old traditional Amana Colonies finishing techniques in his shop.

The Super-Schanz four-coat, hand-rubbed varnish system, as applied today, may sound complicated. But break it down into steps and the complexity disappears. Norman says that anyone with a little patience can get the same good results he and his employees do. In fact, he feels so positive about this that he offers his custom-blended sealer and varnishes to do-it-yourselfers and provides the necessary step-by-step instructions. (See our Buying Guide for details.)

No glass-slick sanding in this shop

Here's the very first departure from typical woodworking proce-dures we spotted in the Schanz shop—no elaborate or extra-smooth sanding. In preparing wood for finishing, most woodworkers sand with progressively finer and finer sandpaper to end up with an ultra-smooth surface. Not here! At Schanz's, each piece gets sanded once, usually on the stroke sander or one of the drum sanders. And, it's done with 60-grit paper!

"We don't waste time sanding to a glass-slick surface before applying the finish—the results won't be any better," Schanz admonishes. "Leaving the surface this coarse gives the sealer a better bite so it adheres better to the wood's sur-face." Actually, we noted this sand-ing produces a surface comparable to what you'd get hand-sanding with 100-grit sandpaper.

Building the finish, coat by coat

Schanz's four-coat, hand-rubbed varnish system consists of one coat of varnish sanding sealer, two coats of gloss varnish, and a final coat—usually a satin varnish.

"We spray our special varnish-based sanding sealer for the first coat," Norman explains. "It has equal parts of varnish and sand-ing sealer. It seals and builds film at the same time. We apply it with no thinning, as heavy as possible, almost to the point of runoff."

This multicoat system requires sanding after applying each coat. "We sand just enough to level the surface for the next coat," says Norman. "Of course, you have to remove dirt bumps and take care of runs, if there are any. But other-wise, don't sand away any more of the coat than necessary. You want to build up a level film." He also advises removing the sanding dust.

Another piece of Amana furniture gets the hand-sanded, hand-rubbed treatment from Sue Sherman.

You only get a hand-rubbed look by rubbing

Schanz applies a top coat of satin varnish that gives a reduced sheen. Then comes rubbing.

"We always rub the final coat," Schanz says. "A lot of products advertise that they produce a 'hand-rubbed' look without rubbing, but I've never seen one that looks as good as when you do rub it."

To create that "rubbed look" the Schanz crew rubs the final coat with 0000-grade steel wool. On large surfaces where straight-line air sanders can be used, they'll rub with a nylon pad called Bear-Tex.

"You have to rub until you've dulled the surface uniformly," he advises. "Sometimes you think you're damaging the finish, but you won't if you rub with the wood grain and apply uniform pressure."

Rubbing produces a gray cast on the finish surface. To remove this, the finishers wipe the surface with a rubbing oil similar to lemon oil.
continued

THE TRADITIONAL AMANA FINISH
continued

Walnut, sanded with 60-grit paper, and ready for finishing.

First coat of varnish sanding sealer, dry and ready for sanding.

Final satin-varnish coat, ready for final sanding and rubbing.

Four-coat varnish finish pictured at right fares well in appearance comparison with a lacquer finish pictured at left.

12 easy steps to a fine Amana finish

To reproduce the same tough, protective finish on your wood projects, follow these simple steps:

1. Sand new furniture smooth. Strip old furniture to bare wood and sand.

2. If you stain, brush on, then remove excess, wiping with the grain. Let stain dry at least 24 hours.

3. Apply a uniform coat of varnish sanding sealer, and let dry 24 hours.

4. Sand the sealer with 180-grit sandpaper to remove any runs or dust particles and to level the sealer. Sand only enough to smooth the surface. Remove sanding dust with a tack cloth.

5. Apply the first coat of gloss varnish, and let dry 24 hours.

6. Sand the gloss coat with 180-grit sandpaper to level the film's surface. Remove the sanding dust.

7. Apply the second coat of gloss varnish, and let dry at least 24 hours.

8. Sand the second gloss coat lightly with 220-grit sandpaper. Remove all sanding dust.

9. Apply the satin-varnish topcoat. Dry thoroughly, preferably for several days.

10. Sand the satin topcoat lightly with 320-grit sandpaper. Remove all sanding dust.

11. Rub surface with 0000-grade steel wool until a dull-looking sheen or gray cast appears. Apply uniform pressure, and rub with the grain. You can use Bear-Tex or a similar rubbing pad in place of the steel wool.

12. Clean the surface with lemon oil. Periodically reapply lemon oil to renew the finish. Sit back and enjoy your work.

"We used to brush all of our finishes," says Schanz. "But to stay competitive, we've had to adapt new techniques. So we bought the sprayer. It not only saves us time but also yields a better finish."

Schanz uses an airless-spray system. The operator, Sue Sherman, follows a set pattern or sequence when spraying each piece of furniture and uses a turntable and spray racks when possible. Spraying a rocking chair, for example, takes her about 40 seconds.

"In our shop, the spray operator also sands," quips Norman, "so she gets to see the job she's doing. But, Sue does a good job," he adds.

You can brush-apply the finish, and Norman recommends it for small projects. He says to just load the brush often, flow on the varnish, and try to get the coat as uniform as possible.

Schanz batches all finishing operations—spraying every Friday. Each piece sprayed that day gets the same application. For example, on one Friday, Sue sprays sealer. These items dry over the weekend and will be sanded the following week. The following Friday, the next coat will be applied. This sequence continues through the cycle, then starts over again.

Buying Guide

• **Schanz sanding sealer, gloss varnish, satin varnish.** For current prices of pint cans, contact Schanz Furniture & Gift Shop, Highway 6, South Amana, IA 52334, or call 319-622-3529.

• **Norton Bear-Tex.** Nonwoven nylon impregnated with aluminum oxide or silicon carbide. Norton Company, Abrasives Marketing Group, 1 New Bond Street, Box 15008, Worcester, MA 01615-0008. Call 508-795-5000 for prices.

WATER-BASED FINISHES

You say you don't know the first thing about water-based finishes? Well, you're not alone. Until recently, very few people other than professional floor finishers were aware of the easy water cleanup, low odor, clarity, and fast-drying nature of these finishes. That, coupled with two notable drawbacks—grain-raising and high cost—kept them out of the hands of most home woodworkers.

But today, with improvements in the performance and availability of these finishes, and governmental pressure for environmentally friendly coatings, water-based finishes have officially "arrived" for home woodworkers.

In light of these happenings, we decided the time was right for us to take a close look at today's water-based finishes. So, we rounded up most of the major brands and tried them out. Now we're ready to tell you what to expect with these products, and how to make them work for you.

How water-based finishes work

What makes water-based finishes so different from the solvent-based products you're used to? Two things actually. The first has to do with the makeup of the finishes. Solvent-based finishes contain anywhere from 50 to 80 percent solvents (often referred to as petroleum distillates or mineral spirits) and 20 to 50 percent solids. Solids are the ingredients left on the wood after the solvents evaporate. Water-based finishes, on the other hand, contain more than 60 percent water, about 30 to 40 percent solids, and only 3 to 10 percent solvents. So, when a water-based finish dries, mostly water—and only a small amount of environment-damaging solvents—goes into the air.

We finished a red-oak board with a water-based coating (*left*) and an oil-based polyurethane (*right*). Note that the water-based finish left a transparent film on the board surface.

The other thing you need to know about water-based finishes is that they dry transparent. The reason: These products don't contain linseed, tung, or other oils that typically give solvent-based coatings an amber coloring as shown *above*. If you want to achieve this warm, yellow look with water-based finishes, you need to stain the surface with light amber stains.

As we found out at an early stage in our research, manufacturers label many water-based products as either *polyurethanes* or *lacquers*, even though the finishes bear little resemblance to solvent-based polyurethanes or nitrocellulose lacquers. Some companies, such as Flecto and Basic Coatings, simply refer to water-based products as *coatings* or *finishes*.

Amity sells both "lacquer" and "polyurethane" water-based finishes. Their labeling was explained this way: "We use the terms lacquer and polyurethane so customers can relate to the products they are replacing. Like solvent-based polyurethane, our water-based polyurethanes contain urethane, provide a tough finish, and cost a little more than our lacquers."

continued

WATER-BASED FINISHES
continued

What's behind the move to water-based finishes

Ever since major California air districts limited volatile organic compounds (VOC) in finishing products during the 1960s, manufacturers have researched low-VOC coatings.

Today, a majority of states have strict requirements for VOC control.

Manufacturers can meet these requirements in one of two ways: Either reduce the level of solvents in their solvent-based finishes, or switch to water-based finishes. Today, manufacturers follow both routes, but most of the company representatives we spoke to felt that only water-based finishes hold the key to meeting ever-tightening VOC regulations.

Our assessment: How the finishes perform

After trying water-based finishes on a variety of projects, we've decided to use these products in the *WOOD*® magazine shop whenever practical. But, we're not ready to entirely drop solvent-based finishes from our shop yet. Why? On many projects, especially intricate ones, we'll still use lacquers and polyurethanes to completely seal the wood grain before applying a water-based finish.

To make a personal decision, you need to weigh the advantages and disadvantages against your own needs. To help you out, we've come up with the report card *above right.* If you decide to make the switch to water-based finishes, give yourself a little time to get used to these products, and put in some practice on scrap wood before tackling an actual project. And, don't forget to take the same safety precautions with these products that you would with solvent-based finishes. Once dry, these finishes burn every bit as well as the residues of solvent-based products.

Water-Based Finishes

Subject	Grade	Comments
Clarity	A	Absolutely clear. Great if you want a transparent finish. Not so great if you want a warm glow in the wood.
Cleanup	A+	Enough said.
Cost	E	Expensive—costs nearly twice as much as oil-based finishes.
Drying Speed	A	Fast. Sometimes too fast.
Grain Raising	D	Lots of room for improvement here.
Hardness	A	Finish can be rubbed out and polished after drying for one day.
Odor	A	Little odor.
Bubbling	C	Harder to control than most solvent-based finishes.

10 steps to a successful water-based finish

Before starting our tests, we gathered samples from nine manufacturers including the suppliers of the five products shown *below*. We also tested finishes from Basic Coatings (Professional Image finishes), Hydrocote, Minuteman Furniture Restoration Systems, and Wood-Kote. All of the coatings performed acceptably. Amity and Hydrocote have the widest ranges of products, including stains, fillers, sanding sealers, and rubbing compounds. At this point, only Hydrocote produces exterior- and marine-grade water-based finishes.

After two months of testing, we've developed a series of application steps to guide you. We worked mostly with red oak because its open grain structure poses more challenges to the water-based finishes than tighter-grained woods such as walnut or cherry. Here's how to go about it:

1. Get the right product. Some finishes are formulated exclusively for spraying, so look for a product intended for brushing if you don't have a spray gun. The brushable coatings have flow-out and debubbling agents not found in the spray-only finishes. Remember to read the application instructions carefully.

2. Stir the finish. This disperses the leveling, debubbling, and flow agents that help the finish perform as well as possible. Don't shake the container—you'll just create more bubbles.

3. Wet the wood surface. To help you deal with the tendency of water-based finishes to raise wood grain, wet the wood with plain water as shown before you put together the project. This way, you can sand the pieces as described in the next step without manipulating the sandpaper into tight spots created by assembly. A sponge or rag works well, but remember to apply just enough water to raise the grain without soaking the surface.

4. Sand the raised grain. With a finish sander or hand block, smooth the surface with a succession of 150- and 220-grit sandpapers as shown *opposite*. Thoroughly clean all sanding dust from the surface with an air hose or vacuum. Don't use a tack cloth—it may contain waxes or oils not compatible with water-based finishes.

5. If desired, stain the surface. Even after following the above steps, a water-based stain or finish will still raise the grain, especially on open-grained woods. This

Apply a thin film of water with a sponge or rag to raise the grain.

Sand the surface smooth with 150- and 220-grit sandpaper.

increases your odds of sanding off the stain when smoothing successive finish coats. So if your test pieces reveal a problem here, we suggest you stick to oil-based stains. Several manufacturers, including Deft and Flecto, produce oil-based stains that clean up with water and release negligible odor. These stains will seal the surface partially, reducing or eliminating raised grain on successive coats of clear finish. Gelled stains, such as those sold by Wood-Kote, do an even better job of sealing the wood. However, these products do not clean up with water. And, if you choose an oil-based stain, make certain the stain has dried completely before applying a water-based finish.

6. Strain the finish. In our tests, chunks of coagulated coating occasionally accumulated inside the containers of the water-based finishes. These chunks were the number one culprit in surface blemishes. To eliminate this problem, pour the finish into a clean second container through a cone-type strainer or nylon stocking as shown on *page 58*.

7. If possible, use a sanding sealer. Amity, Hydrocote, and Minuteman sell water-based sanding sealers, and we highly recommend these for your first coat or two. These sealers build more quickly than the finishes, and also sand much more easily.

8. Brush on the finish. To keep bubbles to a minimum, use a high-quality, clean, nylon/poly-ester brush. Dip it no more than 1" or so into the strained liquid to prevent overloading the brush. After completing your work, you can pour any remaining strained finish back into the container supplied by the manufacturer.

Since heavy coats raise the grain of bare wood more than thin coats, apply a thin first coat. This coat will seal the grain and allow you to apply heavier successive coats. Minimize your brush strokes over already-wetted areas.

continued

WATER-BASED FINISHES
continued

An old nylon stocking helps you strain coagulated chunks and other debris from the finish. You can also purchase cone-shaped strainers just for this purpose.

On contoured surfaces, smooth the finish with 3M Scotchbrite pads instead of steel wool.

9. Allow the coats to dry thoroughly. Although the finish may feel dry after only 15 minutes, allow each coat to dry at least one hour before applying the next. Otherwise, you may seal moisture beneath your topcoats, leaving the finish with a milky appearance. You can reduce drying times with a fan or hair dryer set on low heat to speed evaporation. Be careful. Overheating may cause blisters.

10. Sand between successive coats. After sanding your first coat with 220-grit sandpaper, brush on following coats as described in Step 7. Because of the high solid content of water-based finishes, even thin coats build fast and provide a tough protective layer.

For irregular surfaces, such as the table leg shown *below left,* smooth between coats with a fine 3M Scotchbrite pad. Steel wool does not work because any bits of the steel left on the wood surface will rust. Steel screws will rust, too.

Points to keep in mind for spraying

If you can afford it, a spray system produces the best possible results with water-based finishes. In our trials, the coatings worked equally well with conventional spray guns and the new high-volume, low-pressure (HVLP) systems designed to minimize overspray.

With a conventional system, we had our best results at 20 psi and a 6–8" spray pattern. Keep in mind that you must thoroughly clean water-based finishes from all parts of your gun to prevent rusting and finish buildup. We noticed that the coatings formed a skin over the nozzle if the gun was left to sit for just a few minutes. So, do as much spraying as possible in one session, then immediately clean the gun thoroughly with water.

After rolling on the finish, smooth it by lightly dragging a brush across the surface.

Conventional spray systems waste more than half of your finish by dispersing it into the air (mostly in the form of overspray), so manufacturers have developed HVLP machines that place 70–80 percent of the finish on the workpiece. The result: less pollution and nearly twice the finish-transfer efficiency. If you already own a compressor, you can purchase a stand-alone turbine sprayer. The turbine feeds a stream of warm air to the gun at about 5 psi.

How to cover a large surface

To quickly and effectively finish tabletops, doors, or other large surfaces, professionals often employ this trick. First, roll a thin, uniform layer of finish onto the surface with a ¼ "-nap roller. Then, lightly drag a high-quality brush across the wet finish as shown *above* to even out the coating and eliminate bubbles.

On surfaces of more than 2 square feet or so, we also had good luck with short-hair painting pads.

These handy applicators quickly put a thin, even layer of finish over a 6–8"-wide surface. Try to simply lay the finish down and not repad it.

Water-based products dry quickly, so you won't have time to rebrush the finish. Keeping that in mind, carefully plan how you'll finish the project before getting started.

DECORATIVE AND SPECIAL-PURPOSE FINISHES

Crackled, marble, color, or dye—with special finishes you can transform any piece into something unique. Here, you'll learn how to age a surface 100 years and provide a weatherproof finish to keep tomorrow's antiques looking brand new.

MODERN-DAY CRACKLING

Decades ago, the accidental mixing of the wrong paint and varnish ingredients produced startling results better suited to alligators than fine furniture. Even so, the crackled effect had a charm of its own, creating a striking finish of contrasting colors.

Today, you can achieve a crackled finish on wood (and on other materials as well) from a two-spray-can kit made by Plasti-Kote. When testing the kit, we had to practice before we felt comfortable using the two components. But once mastered, the kit gave us impressive crackled surfaces that promised lots of possibilities.

Take a pop at crackling— it's a snap

To try your hand at crackling, first prepare a clean, smooth, sanded surface. Then, seal the bare wood with a lacquer-based primer.

Next, spray on the colored base coat, applying the material evenly as you hold the spray nozzle about 8" away from the surface. Since this is a spray lacquer, it will dry quickly. Build up a uniform base coat by spraying on three or four layers. Allow 30 minutes to dry.

After finishing the last base layer, allow the surface to dry. (We waited an hour or so.) Then, apply the topcoat, which comes in a contrasting color. For a small crackling pattern, we completely covered the base coat with one layer of the topcoat. For a medium pattern, we made two passes over the surface. And for large crackles, we found that four consecutive passes did the trick, creating a heavy top layer. Thick layers of both base and topcoats assure coarse crackling.

Within a few minutes after applying the topcoat, you'll be amazed as you watch the finish begin to crack and shrink, exposing the base layer. You'll probably produce a finish that isn't uniformly crackled all over, but that's part of the fun and intrigue.

Five helpful hints

• For the best results, apply Cracklin' Finish when room, paint, and project temperatures are between 60 and 85 degrees. And be sure you're in a well-ventilated area, away from open flames or other fire hazards for a safe, worry-free application.

• Experiment on scrap with this unusual product before applying it to your project.

• You cannot switch colors by applying the topcoat first and covering it with a layer of base coat. That's because the base coat contains the chemicals that make the topcoat crackle.

• This finish appears textured, but don't be fooled. It's plenty smooth enough for most uses.

• Indoor accent pieces like those pictured *opposite* are perfect for this finish, but the manufacturer says it's durable enough for outdoor projects, too.

Your color options

Cracklin' Finish comes in black on white, white on black, black on red, black on gold, gray on black, and white on gold antique. The 12-ounce cans of base coat and topcoat will cover 18 to 25 square feet. And though we only tried the product on wood, the manufacturer says it also works on metal, glass, and plastic.

Note: *For more information, call Plasti-Kote Cracklin' Finish at 800-431-5928.*

PAINTED STONE FINISHES

2. With a high-quality nylon polyester brush, apply successive coats of Amity white primer to the workpiece until the surface appears totally white (see the Buying Guide for a source of supplies). Each coat should dry in about one hour, but we decreased the drying time to 15 minutes with the aid of a hair dryer set on *low* as shown in photo B. Sand lightly between coats with 220-grit paper.

3. With a square stick of soft, compressed black charcoal, draw surface veins that look like concrete cracks or bolts of lightning. Draw the veins at a 45° angle across the surface as shown in photo C. For a natural effect, apply light pressure to the charcoal, and try to shake your hand somewhat. Resharpen the charcoal stick now and then by dragging its tip across sandpaper.

A

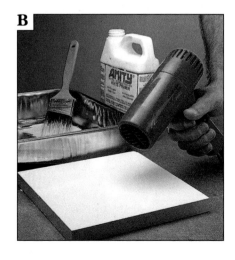
B

Chicago-based woodworker Bill Aitchison sent *WOOD*®'s products editor the handsome little dish shown *above.* What's most impressive is that he turned it from particleboard and painted it to look like marble and granite. As an experiment, we set the dish on a desk to see how many people it would fool. One after another, members of the *WOOD*® magazine staff picked up the dish, only to be amazed at its light weight and particleboard construction. When Bill told us that anybody could learn to perform this wood-into-stone magic in a few hours with fast-drying water-based paints, we had to know more.

Step-by-step to a rock-solid marble look

After just three practice pieces, we produced the granite-and-marble tabletop shown *above.* After you learn to marbleize, we'll walk you through the steps for a granitelike finish.

1. Because of the strong adhesion qualities of water-based products, these procedures work well on most any material. (For the tabletop *above,* we chose particleboard because it cuts and shapes easily, and has a smooth surface.) After machining your pieces, be sure to fill all cut edges with putty as shown in photo A, and sand flat the filled areas with 150-grit sandpaper.

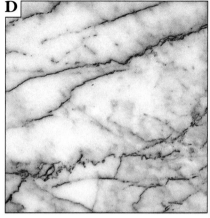

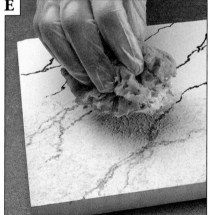

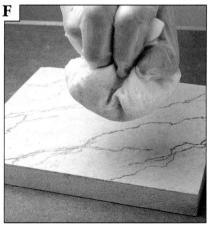

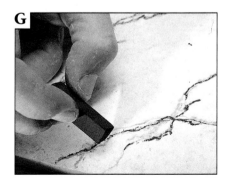

This and the following two steps require some practice and patience, but your rate of improvement will amaze you. As you practice, pay attention to the pattern of the veins in the piece of genuine Palomino marble shown in photo D.

4. Dip a piece of natural sponge with torn (not cut) faces into a shallow pan of Amity white primer, and lightly dab the entire work surface (in a random pattern) as shown in photo E. The sponge will pick up some of the charcoal and spread it around the surface to blend the veins with the background. Lift the sponge straight up and down so you don't smudge the charcoal. Re-wet the sponge after 10 or 12 dabs.

5. Fold a clean cotton rag that has little pattern or "weave" (a worn diaper works fine) so it fits into your hand and has no wrinkles on its bottom side. With this pad, blot the entire surface as shown in

photo F to further blend the charcoal and paint. Again, be careful to lift the rag straight up and down.

Note: *Because water-based paints dry quickly, don't waste any time between Steps 4 and 5. It helps to prefold the rag and set it aside before starting Step 4.*

6. After the paint dries, again dip the sponge into the white primer and sparingly dab small, random areas of the surface. Try to "bury" portions of the veins and lighten the larger white areas between the veins. This and the following step add depth and realism to the marble. Reblot the surface with a rag as described in Step 5.

7. Accentuate the veins by slightly darkening about half of them with charcoal as shown in photo G. Lightly sponge and blot the surface as described earlier in Steps 4 and 5.

8. To make the surface look like polished marble, apply at least three
continued

PAINTED STONE FINISHES
continued

coats of a gloss water-based finish such as Amity gloss lacquer. (For more information on water-based finishes, see *page 55*.)

Granite: The perfect complement to the marble look

The granitelike effect makes a great border or trim for a marbleized surface. As you work, strive for a mottled look of black, gray, and white specks.

1. Prepare and prime the surface as described in Steps 1 and 2 in the marbleizing section. Into a shallow pan, pour separate pools (about 1 ounce each) of Amity black and white primer.

2. Dip a natural sponge into the black primer and lightly dab the entire surface as shown in photo H. Apply the black randomly and sparingly, being careful to move the sponge straight up and down.

3. With some black paint still on the sponge, immediately dip it into the white primer and mix the two colors in another area of the pan as shown in photo I. Dab the surface with this mixture as shown in photo J.

4. Blot the surface as described in Step 5 of the marbleizing procedure. By this point, you should have a surface that appears to be a random mix of black, gray, and white specks. If you're not satisfied, just responge the surface.

5. Add a clear finish as described in Step 8 of the marbleizing technique.

Buying Guide
•**Faux stone kit,** including one pint each of black and white paints, natural sponge, and charcoal. One quart of brushable clear lacquer (specify satin or gloss). For current prices, call Amity at 608-837-8484.

HOME BREWS OF NONTOXIC FINISHES AND REMOVERS

With a little effort, you can concoct some friendly, nonpolluting mixtures to perform a number of chores.

Paint you can make

Toxic chemicals and carcinogens abound in paints, especially those that are petroleum based. To stem possible pollution, most landfills won't accept paint cans—you have to take empties (even latex-based) to a hazardous-waste disposal site. But you do have an option.

Milk paint was a popular and safe colorant a century ago, and it's still an easy-to-make, inexpensive alternative. To get the old-time look on some of your woodworking projects, try this formula: Mix enough hot water with instant, nonfat dry milk to form a smooth syrup. Add small amounts of powdered tempera color (available at art-supply and paint stores) to get the shade you want. Apply in coats for a rich, flat finish. Although milk paint does dry more slowly than store-bought, it's very durable and has an authentic Early American look.

Need to remove paint?

If you don't mind mixing and a slower pace, we discovered an inexpensive, odorless, and nontoxic formula for paint remover that's nearly as effective as what you can buy. Mix 1 pound of trisodium phosphate (TSP), a natural cleansing powder derived from minerals that you can obtain at paint and hardware stores, into 1 gallon of hot water. (Be sure to wear rubber gloves; TSP can irritate your skin.) Then, brush on the mixture and let it sit for 30 minutes. Remove the softened paint with a scraper. Of course, multiple coats of paint require repeated applications.

Two surefire ways to soften brushes

Here again, you can turn to trisodium phosphate. Add 4 ounces of TSP to 1 quart of hot water. Work the solution into the bristles by pressing them against the bottom of the container, then separate them as the paint softens. When all paint has been removed, rinse with water. This process takes longer than with the traditional high-powered commercial product, but it's a lot more pleasant.

Over time, we've found that vinegar rates a place in everyone's shop. It not only removes fresh epoxy from fingers and material, and loosens old glue, but it also softens paint (even tough milk paint). To clean brushes, pour enough distilled white vinegar (5 percent acid) into an old saucepan to cover the bristles. Bring it to a boil on the stove, then reduce the heat and let it simmer for five minutes. When the brushes cool, wash them in soap and water, then rinse thoroughly.

Citrus to the rescue

Take the old household hint about removing stains with lemon juice a step further. Believe it or not, you can clean and shine metals with a plain lemon. For brass, use straight lemon juice (fresh or reconstituted). Copper cleans better when you add a few sprinkles of salt to the juice. In both instances, rinse the juice off the metal with water after cleaning. Don't use lemon juice on silver or gold; it can stain.

COUNTRY FINISHES

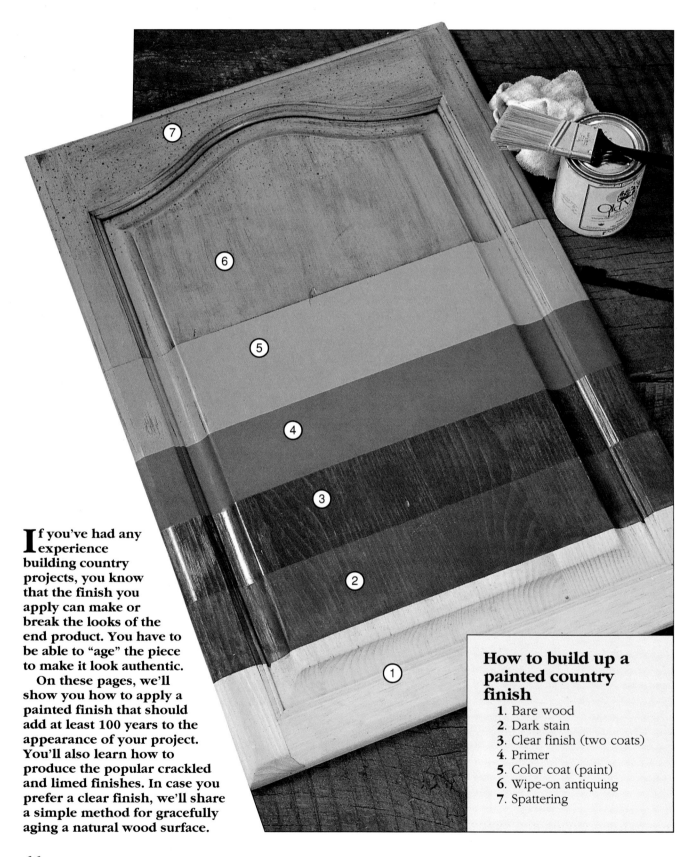

If you've had any experience building country projects, you know that the finish you apply can make or break the looks of the end product. You have to be able to "age" the piece to make it look authentic.

On these pages, we'll show you how to apply a painted finish that should add at least 100 years to the appearance of your project. You'll also learn how to produce the popular crackled and limed finishes. In case you prefer a clear finish, we'll share a simple method for gracefully aging a natural wood surface.

How to build up a painted country finish

1. Bare wood
2. Dark stain
3. Clear finish (two coats)
4. Primer
5. Color coat (paint)
6. Wipe-on antiquing
7. Spattering

Most of the finishing experience we have here at *WOOD*® magazine centers around clear finishes. Usually, we like to let the wood show itself off—naturally.

But country finishes are a different matter. And frankly, until recently we didn't know much about the topic. But that was before we met up with Dick Fitch, a master of the art, who consults with the people at the Bartley Collection, Ltd., a woodworking-kit manufacturer and finish formulator in Easton, Maryland. With more than a half-century of experience in paint and other finishes, Dick is a veritable storehouse of knowledge on the subject.

Now that we've spent two days working alongside Dick in his shop, and several more experimenting in our own, we're finally ready to show you what we've discovered about these interesting and not-too-difficult techniques.

Five easy steps to a painted antique finish

1. Distress the unpainted surface. Antiques usually have their fair share of dings, nicks, and scratches. But, before you go out blemishing the surface of your new project, imagine where the object would have received the greatest

For an edge-rounding tool, wrap 80-grit sandpaper around a 1" dowel.

wear through the years. Then, plan your distressing accordingly. You can use a ball peen hammer to simulate dents, a screwdriver to make scratches, and a rasp to scuff heavily used areas. Then, gently round the edges and corners with 80-grit sandpaper wrapped around a 1" dowel as shown *below left*. For a natural "worn" look, remember to sand the edges unevenly from spot to spot.

And, don't overdo it. If a surface would have received little wear over the years, leave it alone. As Dick Fitch told us: "You want to distress—not destroy."

2. Apply the finish in layers as shown in the photo *opposite*. This process yields great results, but it does require up to seven coats of finishes. So, be patient. As you'll see in Step 3, these multiple layers will lead to the aged look you're after.

To start, wipe on a dark stain and let dry. Then, apply two protective layers of a clear finish (preferably polyurethane), and lightly sand the second coat before laying down a primer paint. The primer can be any paint, but it should be close in color to one of the favorite colonial primer colors: iron-oxide red (our favorite), black, or mustard yellow.

After the primer dries, follow up with the color coat. (The earthy hues shown at *right* look great on country projects.)

Latex and oil-based paints work fine, and you can apply one over the other. However, always sand an oil-based paint before applying a latex finish over it. Otherwise, the latex material may pool or not adhere properly.

3. Now, roll back the years by using 320-grit sandpaper to wear away the color coat along edges, corners, and other areas where the paint would have worn off through use. Although 320-grit paper loads up fast, a coarser paper cuts too quickly through the various layers. First, lightly sand the entire surface, *continued*

Dressing-table blue**

Peacock plume*

Newport blue*

Teal stencil*

Saltbox blue*

Soldier blue**

Arcadian*

Village green*

Shaker red*

Cajun red*

New England red**

You can purchase paints in the colors shown on this page from these sources:
***Heritage colors available from Sherwin Williams. See your local dealer.**
****The Stulb Paint Company. Call 800-221-8444 for the dealer nearest you.**

COUNTRY FINISHES
continued

then sand down to the primer coat around hard-use areas as shown *below*. If you should accidentally sand through the primer, the two clear coats will protect the stained wood. Since old wood is darker than new wood, try not to reveal the bare wood.

320-grit sandpaper helps you remove the color coat without sanding through the primer.

4. **Patina in five minutes?** Sure! Just apply a coat of dark oil-based gel stain over the surface, then wipe away most of it with a lint-free cloth as shown *below*. Leave deposits in crevices and other areas not likely to have received wear and cleaning over the years. The residue left behind after you remove the stain

To simulate patina, leave accumulations of a dark gel stain in the nooks and crannies of the surface.

simulates the buildup of grime referred to as "patina." For a source of gel stain, see *page 70*.

5. Add a bit more character by spattering the surface. To achieve this accent (called "fly specks" by some), first mix two parts gel stain with one part mineral spirits in a shallow container. Then, dab an old toothbrush, or a paintbrush with its bristles trimmed to ½ " long, into the mixture. Practice your spattering technique on a piece of paper before trying it on your project. Place the brush about 6" from the paper, and run your finger through the bristles. When you feel you have the right touch, add a uniform spattering of fine speckles to the workpiece as we're doing *below*. Don't overdo it. A little spattering goes a long way.

Note: *Spattering and antiquing work well on nonwood surfaces, too.*

The crackled look

No painted surface looks as old as one that has crackled. This process can take decades to occur naturally, but this method requires only a few days.

After practicing your spattering technique on paper, give the project a uniform coat of fine speckles.

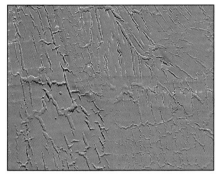

A crackled finish made with latex paints over hide glue and (*left*) a crackled surface covered with an oil-based paint

First give the project a base coat of paint if you don't want bare wood to show between the crackles. After this coat dries, brush on a thin, uniform coat of hide glue over any areas that you want to crackle. The hide glue must dry thoroughly, and this may take a day or more. Then, apply latex paint in long, even strokes. In 20 to 30 seconds, the paint will begin to crackle. We achieved the effect *above, top* by skipping the first coat of paint and applying hide glue over bare wood, followed with coats of white and green paint.

Once again, it pays to experiment in order to achieve just the effect you want. If you prefer a more subtle crackling, use the above procedure, but cover the latex coat with oil-based paint, as we did in the example *above.* Because the oil-based paint doesn't crackle, it covers the surface completely.

The limed look

When *WOOD*® magazine's design editor, Jim Downing, visited an international furniture show in High Point, North Carolina, he reported seeing a lot of pine furniture with a limed finish. The pieces looked as if they had been painted white and then partially stripped. We investigated the liming process, and found it surprisingly simple.

Paint: The finish of choice for 18th-century Americans

During colonial times, most citizens painted their furniture. Why? Paints cost less than clear finishes of the day, and applied quicker and easier. Also, furniture was often made from several wood species that would not stain evenly.

For instance, the classic Windsor chair was often made from as many as four different woods. The spindles and legs might be made of oak or maple, the bent back from hickory or ash, and the seat from pine. Imagine trying to stain such a chair evenly!

As you can see by the side-by-side comparison *below,* this procedure adds a soft elegance to pine. Open-grain woods, such as oak, soak up more paint, making them look even whiter.

Oil-based paint works best for liming because its longer drying period gives you more working time. To get a shade of white that *continued*

Liming (*above left*) gives wood a partially stripped look.

COUNTRY FINISHES
continued

Accentuate knots by cutting a shallow, paint-holding crevice with an X-acto knife or similar tool.

suits your taste, experiment by mixing small amounts of black, green, yellow, and other colors into a pure-white base. Also, practice this technique on scrap stock before you lime your project.

To start, brush white paint over the entire surface and wipe it off of the high areas, leaving paint in the crevices and corners. For an added effect, next use a small brush to place more paint in all the crevices, being careful to feather the new paint into the old.

If you want to make the piece look even older, score around the knots with an X-acto knife prior to painting as shown *above*. Use the same knife to open up glue joints slightly—the extra paint will accentuate the crevices.

Tips on creating a natural antique finish

To make a natural wood surface look old, follow these steps:

1. Distress the piece just as described on *page 67*, keeping in mind that the surface will look

older and older with every scratch, nick, and dent.

2. Apply a dark stain to areas such as the bases of legs and other places along edges where dirt would likely accumulate over time as shown *below*. Add the same stain to scratches and nicks to accentuate these blemishes. Again, we prefer gel stains for greater controllability.

3. Apply a lighter stain to the remaining areas, and blend the stains where they meet. Let both stains sit for a few minutes, then wipe away the excess.

4. Lighten heavily worn areas with paint thinner before the stain dries. As shown at *bottom,* we lightened the areas of the foot stool where shoes would have likely worn off the finish. To add highlights along edges and corners, sand lightly with 320-grit paper. Now, you can add spatters and a clear coat of your choice.

Buying Guide
• **Gel stain.** For a free catalog, write The Bartley Collection, 29060 Airpark Drive, Easton, MD 21601.

Apply a dark gel stain to areas prone to dirt buildup.

Before the stain dries, lighten any high-wear areas with paint thinner.

FINISHING PINE FOR AN EARLY AMERICAN LOOK

Much of pine's beauty comes from the patina it builds up over the years. But what about that new pine project you're planning? Here's how to give it an old-pine look.

Although you'll never duplicate the wonderful patina of a 200-year-old, museum-quality pine piece, you can greatly enhance the appearance of a new pine project by giving it a special, Early American, mellow look. There are several ways to approach it: Start with the right (and more expensive) kind of pine, or use a lesser-grade pine and finish the piece with some proven tricks.

The best wood makes it easier

Selecting the right wood, such as white western pine, does wonders from the beginning. Usually, this pine is called "Idaho white pine," and carries the initials "IWP" in the grade stamp on every board. White eastern pine and sugar pine will also work. Look for these pines in small, independent lumberyards or those catering to cabinetmakers. You can also special-order them.

How to mellow the yellow

If you want to use less expensive, construction-grade pines—ponderosa, lodgepole, or southern yellow—you'll need to work some finishing magic. That's because these yellow pines have alternating soft, then hard, grains that end up looking like a zebra when they're stained.

To mellow the stain on yellow pine, you need to cut down on how much the soft grain absorbs it,

and increase the hard grain's ability to hold it. And that's not as difficult as it sounds.

To reduce the soft grain's porosity, give the raw wood surface a quick coat of ordinary 3-pound shellac diluted 50/50 with denatured alcohol, *before* sanding. Be sure to make it a light coat.

After the shellac dries, sand it lightly with 120-grit sandpaper, then apply the stain. The shellac penetrates deeply into the soft grain, reducing its ability to absorb the stain. At the same time, the light sanding removes the shellac from the hard grain, letting it absorb stain. This technique mutes high contrast, but it has two drawbacks: First, you must spend more time on finishing; second, clogging the soft wood with shellac makes the dark, old-pine look more difficult to achieve. The finish never looks dark enough, no matter how many coats of stain you apply. But, it's close.

Treat the wood roughly

This second technique uses no shellac precoat. Instead, you first sand with no finer than 80-grit sandpaper, then apply your stain.

Strange as it sounds, it's better to omit fine sanding. On yellow pines, you want to rough up the wood, not smooth it down.

Using coarse sandpaper leaves fine grooves on the hard grain that capture stain and lessen contrast. Both the sand-and-shellac technique and this one avoid stain contrast, but only the rough-sanding procedure allows you to darken the wood as much as you want for an Early American look. However, even that takes a special touch

Stains make a difference, too

To cover the hard grain and cut down the contrast, use a muddy, heavily pigmented, dark brown stain with a reddish hue. This helps mask the yellow tint of yellow pines, and creates a warm, orange highlight in the finish.

You'll want to leave some of the stain's pigment on the wood's surface, so allow an extra day of drying time. If you don't, the first coat of sealer you put on may pick up the pigment and move it around. The result? Blotchiness in the stain that'll ruin your project.

Start your finish with orange shellac

Before applying a final, durable varnish, perform one more finishing trick. After the stain has dried thoroughly, put on a couple of full-strength coats of 3-pound orange shellac. Because shellac is alcohol-based, it doesn't usually soften an oil-based stain, and it won't bother a water-based one. It gives your wood the appearance of old-pine patina, and builds up on the surface quickly, adding depth and compensating for the roughness. Without the shellac coating, you'd spend extra time and money on extra coats of varnish.

To complete the Early American look, use a satin rather than a gloss varnish—it makes the grain less obvious. And be sure the varnish will work with the shellac you used. Some varnishes, especially those containing stearic acid, tend to bubble up when put down over shellac. As always, test the varnish and the shellac's compatibility on scrap wood before you begin the finishing.

SEVEN BASIC QUESTIONS AND ANSWERS ABOUT OUTDOOR FINISHES

Unless you like weathered gray—and certainly many folks do—outdoor furniture of redwood, cedar, or treated wood requires a finish. Here's how to choose one that will give your project the look—and protection—you want.

1. Redwood, cedar, and treated wood last and last. So why apply a finish?

An obvious answer is appearance, but there's a practical angle, too.

Redwood and cedar heartwood contain naturally occurring tannic compounds that fend off insects and resist decay. But since they're low in gum and resin and rather open-grained, moisture raises the surface grain and eventually leads to checking and splintering. Mildew then attacks the dampness harbored in the wood.

Pine and hemlock pressure-treated with noncarcinogenic chromated copper arsonate (CCA) chemicals last as long as redwood and cedar. However, treated woods marketed under a variety of brand names still tend to

check. So it's wise to use a moisture-resistant finish.

2. What will outdoor wood look like if left unfinished?

Exposed to the elements, the cinnamon hues of clear all-heart redwood and the cozy brown of cedar turn varying shades of gray. First, though, their tannic compounds leach out somewhat and darken the wood. Depending on conditions, the weathering process can take up to several years.

Wood containing CCA comes with a cast approximating the light green of a dollar bill or, occasionally, an amber color. But treated wood also weathers in a year or two to a pleasing gray.

If you appreciate the weathered look, complete with natural checks and slight surface imperfections (it's very popular on the West Coast), leave your redwood, cedar, or treated wood furniture alone to do its thing.

3. Is it possible to preserve wood's natural color?

If you prefer the natural color of new redwood and cedar to weath-

ered grain, you need a product that leaves a clear surface film on the wood. And that presents a problem.

Clear film finishes protect wood from water while allowing the color to show through, but they admit ultraviolet sun rays. The wood cells react with these rays and begin to deteriorate, causing a minor commotion under the film. The wood darkens and the finish cracks, blisters, and peels.

Adding an ultraviolet (UV) filtering agent to the finish retards the reaction, but doesn't completely do away with it. If you plan to use a clear finish, be sure the one you select has UV absorbers (read the label). Even with UV protection, you'll have to renew the finish at least every two years. If you wait until it peels, you're faced with a tedious stripping job.

With treated wood, you probably won't want to preserve the green color—and that's exactly what happens if you apply a clear finish.

4. What types of clear finishes are there?

Many types of finishes are "clear" in that they carry no color additive, but each looks and performs differently.

• **Spar varnish,** a traditional film treatment, is no doubt the best known product of this type. Others are sold as specially formulated *plastic* or *polyurethane* finishes. Beware of the two-part "mix A and B" polyester coatings when working with redwood and cedar—due to natural extractives in the wood, they won't readily adhere.

• **Oil finishes,** although they do darken the wood noticeably, can also be classified as clear. Because oil finishes penetrate the grain and seal it against the elements rather than create a surface film, they'll never crack, blister, or peel. But they do require touching up every six months or so.

• **Water repellents** are another option. Mixtures of oil and surface film, they penetrate the wood and protect it from moisture damage and mildew. Similar to a surface film, water repellents leave a coating on top of the wood, but most manufacturers add the necessary UV absorbers. You can expect these finishes to last up to two years before they begin to deteriorate and the wood weathers. Then they'll require light sanding before renewal.

• **Paste waxes** usually add only extra protection and sheen to a finish, though at least one manufacturer says two or three coats, rubbed on and renewed, are all that's needed on new wood.

5. Are there differences between opaque and semi-transparent stains?

The breathing ability of pigmented outdoor penetrating stains means the finish won't crack or peel from trapped air, moisture, or possible wood movement. The result is a long-lasting finish with exactly the color tone you want and minimal maintenance.

• **Semi-transparent** stains, with their light pigmentation, let the natural grain and wood texture show through. Such stains are available in colors that very closely match various woods. Brighter colors can either contrast or complement your house, deck, or patio. These stains usually have an oil base.

• **Opaque stains** resemble paint in that they conceal the grain, yet they allow the wood texture to show. They're available in a variety of natural-looking colors and brighter hues, and in both oil and latex base.

Since the pigment in this type of stain is suspended in an oil or latex carrier, it's possible that all wood surfaces won't be equally penetrated. On horizontal surfaces especially, pigment that doesn't completely penetrate may collect, causing blotchy areas that wear off or blister. Also, the California Redwood Association doesn't recommend using stains with a latex base on redwood projects.

Treated lumber, with its greenish hue, requires that you select a compatible stain color, since the green tends to alter the final appearance.

6. When should you use paint?

Paint isn't often used on the top grades of redwood or cedar because it completely hides grain, texture, and color. But it can be your solution to coping with the hue of treated wood.

If you decide to use paint on your outdoor furniture project, no matter what wood you've selected, be sure to apply an oil or alkyd base primer, then sand lightly before finishing, for better adhesion.

You can expect painted furniture's horizontal surfaces to undergo much more wear and tear than vertical surfaces such as house siding, so avoid the need for early renewal or removal by selecting the highest-quality paint available.

7. Does redwood, cedar, or treated wood require special prefinish preparation?

First, any wood has to be clean and dry. Scrub dirty wood with nonammoniated laundry detergent and water, rinse, then let it dry in the sun for a few days.

Sometimes redwood and cedar develop dark discolorations from either mildew or tannic acid, especially if the wood has been outside for awhile. In these cases, scrub affected surfaces with a solution of one cup nonammoniated laundry detergent and one quart of household bleach to three quarts water. Rinse with fresh water, then apply a 50/50 solution of bleach and water. Rinse again and let the wood dry completely. (Be sure to wear rubber gloves and eye protection throughout the process.) To prevent future mildew problems, select a finish containing a mildewcide or use an anti-mildew additive.

To renew severely weathered redwood and cedar, brush away loose wood fibers with a stiff brush, then clean with a mixture of four ounces (dry weight) oxalic acid in a gallon of water. Flush the wood thoroughly with clean water and allow it to dry for several days before finishing.

New treated lumber should be "aged" for 30–60 days before finishing to give the wood time to shed any excess moisture.

Outdoor furniture finishes at a glance					
Finish Type	Appearance	Application	Coats	Renew	Comments
CLEAR: Spar varnish	gloss	brush, spray on	2–3	1–2 yrs.	surface darkens, peels; hard to remove
Polyurethane/ plastic	gloss, semigloss	brush, spray on	2–3	1–2 yrs.	wood darkens, finish cracks; hard to remove
Water repellents	dull sheen	brush/roll on	1–2	2 yrs.	wood eventually darkens; light sanding before renewal
Penetrating oils	dull or flat	wipe on/off	1–2	6 mos.	wood weathers, appears dark; frequent renewal
Paste wax	low sheen	rub on/off	1–2	3–4 mos.	mostly as extra protection; frequent renewal
WEATHERING: Bleaching oils/ stains	flat	brush/wipe on	1-2	1 yr.	wood weathers; ages
COLORED: Semitransparent stains	flat	brush/roll on	1	2 yrs.	grain, texture shows; color fades; wood weathers
Opaque stains	flat	brush/roll on	1	2 yrs.	pigments can blotch, wear off; hides wood features
Paint, (oil, acrylic, latex bases)	flat to high-gloss	brush, roll, spray on	2	2–3 yrs.	needs oil-based primer; can bubble, wear off

Note: This chart applies to outdoor furniture of redwood, cedar, and treated wood. Finishes may perform differently on vertical surfaces such as fences and siding than on horizontal surfaces. Consult a qualified dealer about your specific needs.

A CARVER'S GUIDE TO ACRYLICS

Do your palms start sweating when you lay down the gouges to pick up your paintbrushes? You're not alone. Painting intimidates a lot of carvers. Here's how acrylic paints can help you break out of that crowd and give your carvings the colors they deserve.

Plain old water. That's what makes acrylic paints such a joy to use. You don't need smelly solvents to thin acrylics or clean your brushes—just water.

When you paint with acrylics, you're putting on solid particles of plastic resin and color pigment suspended in water. The water evaporates, drying the paint and leaving the color bonded to the wood in an impermeable acrylic-plastic film.

Dried acrylic paints are waterproof, even washable with soap and water. The colors don't yellow with age, and the flexible coating resists cracking and peeling.

A jarring choice to make

Art-supply and craft shops sell these versatile paints in tubes or jars. Tube acrylics work fine, but for carvings, we prefer the liquid acrylics in jars. Concentrated colors—sold in jars for tole and craft painting—are great for carvings.

Liquid acrylics cover evenly and flow smoothly from the brush so that you can neatly paint fine lines and details. They require less thinning than tube paints, and dry without brush marks, too.

Mix with some big names

You'll find acrylics in scores of colors. However, a dozen or fewer will be enough for most carvers.

When buying colors, look for these standard pigment names to build a basic set: phthalocyanine blue (ask for thalo blue), cadmium red medium, cadmium yellow medium, phthalocyanine green (thalo green), burnt umber, burnt sienna (browns), Mars black, and titanium white. All of these have high tinting strength, which means a little goes a long way in mixing or tinting.

With these basics, you can mix almost any color. To get skin tones, for instance, mix burnt sienna and white. (Some manufacturers sell premixed flesh tones, too.) For guidance in color-mixing, buy a color wheel from your art-supply dealer.

Adding extra colors to your palette widens your range. Some good choices: ultramarine blue, naphthol crimson, permanent green light, and Turner's yellow.

Media sensations

Acrylics thin with water. But beware; too much water weakens the film, allowing the color to rub off. Instead, use polymer medium (or polymer medium and water) to thin an acrylic more than 50 percent. Clear polymer medium—acrylic paint without the pigment—comes in either gloss or matte finish.

Titanium white	Turner's yellow	Burnt sienna	Ultramarine blue	Cadmium yellow medium	Permanent green light

To maintain the acrylics' flat finish, thin with matte medium. Gloss medium increases the shine—handy for adding luster to a figure's belt buckle or buttons, for example. For an overall shine, brush a glaze coat of gloss medium onto the painted carving. For a semigloss coating, mix gloss and matte media.

For an aged appearance, there's crackle medium to craze the painted surface. And you can even patch flaws or build up features with two special media: gel medium and the putty-like acrylic modeling paste, both tintable.

A caution: Before mixing media and paints from different manufacturers, test a small batch. You won't have compatibility problems, though, painting over a dried coat with another brand.

This basic brush set meets most carvers' painting needs. From *left*, the #10 shader, #6 shader, #5 round, #1 liner.

Any old brush will do

Acrylics don't require expensive brushes; any kind will work fine. But do buy at least one high-quality brush that keeps its point and holds paint well. It will take the fear out of painting small details.

Synthetic bristles offer a big plus over natural bristles: Dried acrylics will wash out of them with soap and water. But let acrylics dry in a brush with natural bristles, and you may as well throw it away.

A good starter set for most carvers includes #10 and #6 flat shaders, a #5 round, and a #1 liner. Many dealers sell inexpensive craft brush assortments, which are perfectly suitable.

Get primed for painting

You'll get richer color coats if you first prime the wood with acrylic gesso. That's because bare wood absorbs water from the paints, drying them so fast that brushing on an even coat becomes difficult. Gesso, usually white but available in other colors, seals the wood. It also provides a uniform base coat, eliminating color variations.

For a faded, aged look, apply a transparent wash of thinned acrylic right over bare wood. As an alternative to thinning the paint excessively, tint acrylic natural wood stain with a bit of acrylic color to achieve the effect.

Puttin' on the paints

For easier thinning and mixing when you paint, pour some of each color you're using onto a palette—an old dinner plate or a plastic coffee-can lid will work fine. Spray the palette occasionally with a plant mister to keep the paints from skinning over.

Acrylics dry so quickly that you can lay on multiple coats within minutes of each other. (Force-dry the paint with a hair dryer to speed the process even more.) And, painting over a dried coat won't smear or mix the colors. This makes it easy to correct mistakes; just paint over them.

This fast-drying can work against you sometimes—when you try to blend colors on a wildlife carving, for instance. Keeping the paint and brush wet may allow you enough blending time. (That's another job for your plant mister.) Or, add acrylic retarder to the paint to slow drying.

Acrylics pose one hazard to your personal appearance. When acrylic paint dries on clothes, it can be virtually impossible to remove (acetone does as good a job as anything). So don your grubbies for painting. Or be tidy. While wet, acrylic cleans up with a damp rag or sponge. It washes off skin, wet or dry.

Phthalocyanine green	Naphthol crimson	Mars black	Burnt umber	Phthalocyanine blue	Cadmium red medium

ANILINE DYES

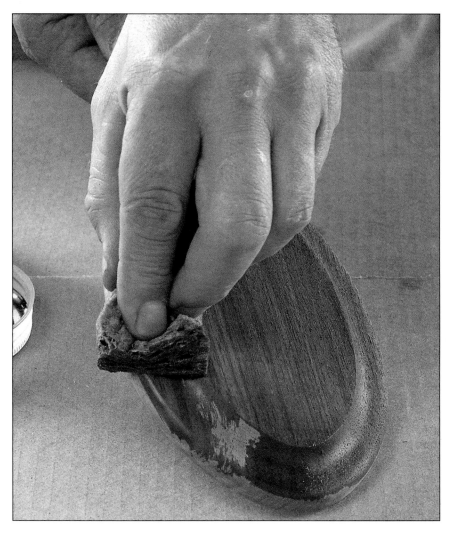

may want to try them all, start with the water-soluble kind. They're easiest to mix (and there's no obnoxious fumes), practically foolproof to use, inexpensive, and come in a rainbow of colors.

Because of the nearly unlimited mixes possible, aniline dyes have been, and continue to be, widely used by professional wood finishers. With six or seven basic colors, a pro can mix and match any wood tone—even peacock blue, if he wants to. In water-soluble anilines, you may choose from over 75 basic colors of powder, and with these you can mix hundreds.

But that doesn't mean you have to mix different-colored powders to arrive at the exact hue you want. To make it easier for you, manufacturers now sell aniline dye powders premixed in wood tones such as Honduras Brown Mahogany, Dark Brown Walnut, or Early American Maple. Of course, you can vary their intensity by adding more water, or change them a bit by tinting with another color. Because anilines are inexpensive, you can afford to experiment.

You'll have few problems with anilines

Water-soluble anilines sometimes get rapped for "raising the grain." And it's true. The water you mix the powder with will cause little hairs of wood fiber to stick up after the dye has dried, requiring some sanding. But, for a really glass-smooth finish, some woodworkers do this sanding anyway, usually after wiping the wood down with water in a prestaining step. Do the same thing and you won't have fuzzy hairs sticking up after you dye the wood.

You might also hear the term "lightfastness" regarding anilines. This refers to the dye's resistance to fading. For all practical purposes, don't worry about it if your project will only be used indoors.

Anilines should only be used on indoor projects. If used on outdoor items, the sun will fade their color.

Just another stain you say? No way! Aniline dyes mix like Kool-Aid, give you clear, deep color that lets the grain show through, and can put savings in your pocket compared to the popular premixed pigmented stains.

How can you color wood for a super look without muddying up the grain? Do as the pros do—try a water-soluble aniline dye on your next project. Here's the difference: Pigmented stains coat the wood with color. The minute, finely ground pigment particles bond to the wood after the carrier (oil, turpentine, solvent, or water) evapo-

rates. All those microscopic pigment bits simply cover up the wood.

On the other hand, aniline dyes completely dissolve—like food coloring—and saturate the wood fibers. The color ends up in the wood, not on it! You see all the grain, like never before.

Perhaps best of all, even amateurs can get professional results the first time. And, anilines are now available from a number of sources listed *opposite*.

Choose colors from a rainbow

Aniline dyes come in powder form, and in three distinct types: water-soluble, alcohol-soluble, and oil-soluble. While eventually you

But indoors, a water-soluble aniline will remain *lightfast* and hold its color for the life of the project.

You also don't have to worry about the color of a water soluble aniline "bleeding" through a clear finish coat. As long as you let the wood dry thoroughly, you can coat it with any finish you choose—from oil to lacquer.

What about safety? Since all anilines come from coal tars through a chemical manufacturing process, use them with commonsense cautions. Don't breathe clouds of the powder, and certainly don't swallow any of the mix. But, at least with the water-soluble kind, there's no need to wear protective gloves or a mask.

How to mix and use water-soluble anilines

If you have mixed Kool-Aid without a hitch, you'll do fine with water-soluble anilines. You need a mixing container, a storage jar, a measuring spoon, a stir stick, and a filter.

To mix a quart of dye, heat up a quart of water to hot (not boiling) temperature. Measure out one ounce of powder for a reasonably concentrated dye (some colors may require a bit more). Then, pour the water into your mixing container and gradually stir in the dye. After dissolving the powder, strain the dye mixture through a filter (a paper coffee filter works perfectly) into a ceramic, plastic, or glass container, such as a canning jar, that you can seal tightly with a lid.

Before dyeing your project, test the color on a scrap of the same wood. Apply with a brush, clean cloth, or sponge. If it's a little dark, add water to the mix. If it's too light, wait until the wood dries, then put on another coat. Or, you can strengthen the mix with some more powder (but reheat the mix before you add powder). When you find a combination that works, note on a piece of paper how you arrived at it—you may want to duplicate the look later.

When you've finished dyeing, cap the dye solution and store it with your other finishing supplies. Kept from freezing, it'll last for years, suffering only from some possible crystallization you cure by reheating the mix. Unmixed, aniline powder stores indefinitely.

Tips from a pro on dyeing wood

We asked John Moser, president of Wood Finishing Supply Co., Inc., Macedon, New York, for some helpful tips for first-timers on using water-soluble anilines. John not only sells the largest selection of aniline dyes we know of, he's also a professional wood finisher with years of experience using nothing but them. Here's what he says:

• **On basic colors for mixing.** "Pros mix all the colors they need from six or seven basic ones. If you want to mix, and it can be fun, buy these five: medium red mahogany, moss green, black, golden oak, and brown walnut. With these, you can match most cabinet woods. Be sure, though, to only mix dissolved colors. Don't try mixing the powders."

• **Getting rid of raised grain.** "Many pros dye the wood first, let it dry completely, then give it a light coat of shellac. It stiffens the hairs so you can sand them off with 220-grit paper for a super smooth finish."

• **Putting on a second coat.** "Always let the wood dry 24 hours after dyeing. If you apply a second coat when the wood is still wet, it won't have an effect."

• **Avoiding lap marks.** "With water-solubles, as long as you keep a 'live edge' of wet dye, you won't get them."

• **Checking color.** "Always go by the wet color of the dye on the wood. As it dries it lightens, but it will come back when you apply the finish."

• **Dyeing softwoods.** "They won't spread evenly on softwood unless you 'size' it first with a mixture of ¼ cup hide glue to one gallon of water. Sand the wood after it dries and before dyeing."

• **Using fillers and dyes.** "Dye open-grain wood first, then seal it with sanding sealer or shellac sealer before filling. This makes a pleasing light/dark contrast. If you fill first, then dye, the filler gets real dark."

Buying Guide

• **Albert Constantine and Son, Inc,** Dept. W, 250 Eastchester Rd., Bronx, NY 10461-2297. 800-223-8087.

• **Garret Wade Company, Inc.,** Dept. W, 161 Ave. of the Americas, New York, NY 10013. 800-221-2942.

• **The Woodworkers Store.** Dept. W, 21801 Industrial Blvd., Rogers, MN 55374-9514. 612-428-3200.

• **Woodcraft Supply Corp.,** 210 Wood County Industrial Park, Box 1686, Parkersburg, WV 26102-1686. 800-225-1153

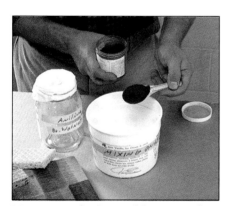

Measure and mix. A tablespoon of aniline powder makes a quart of dye.

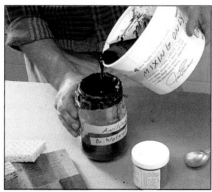

Pour off and strain. A paper filter traps any unmixed powder in the dye solution.

TRY STAIN-RESIST FINISHING

When *WOOD*® magazine reader Dick Link told us about how he was able to place patterns on wood that look like finely placed inlay, we were skeptical. But not any longer! We tested this San Antonian's technique in our shop—and added a couple twists of our own—and we're convinced that this is something worth trying.

Note: *Before trying this technique on your workpiece, practice the procedure on a piece of scrap stock of the same species, with similar grain pattern. Naturally, you don't want to botch your project with a bad finish, so be certain you're pleased with your test piece. We obtained satisfying results with Deft spray stain and Deft clear semigloss lacquer finish, but you may want to experiment with other finishes*

1. Once you've decided on a design that complements your workpiece (we've provided a half-sized pattern *opposite* to get you started), transfer the pattern to a sheet of self-adhesive paper (available from many office-supply stores). Plain-paper copiers provide an easy means to do this, and many machines allow you to reduce or enlarge the image. Or, use carbon paper.

2. Next, seal the self-adhesive sheet by spraying it with two mist coats of lacquer, allowing 5 minutes drying time between applications. The lacquer seal prevents stain from penetrating the sheet and leaving sticky residue on the workpiece. Although the lacquer forms a protective barrier, heavy applications of it may by itself dissolve the adhesive, so go lightly with the lacquer as well as later coats of stain.

3. Finish-sand the project by hand with 150-grit sandpaper, and wipe the surface clean with a tack cloth. Then, peel the backing from your pattern, and apply the sheet onto the work surface. Firmly rub the

pattern down with your hand for strong, even adhesion. With an X-acto knife, carefully cut along the pattern lines as shown, going deep enough to completely cut the paper.

4. With the cutting completed, slowly lift the self-adhesive sheet by one corner and remove it, leaving the pattern adhered to the wood

surface. If part of the design area lifts up because of incomplete cuts, just lower it back to the surface and clip it free with your X-acto knife. Now, with clean hands, rub the segments of the design to make sure they're securely adhered to the wood.

5. Spray a light coat of stain on the entire surface, immediately wipe it with a clean cloth, and let it dry for 5 minutes. If you'd like a darker look, repeat the process as necessary, allowing 5 minutes drying time between coats. For close-grained woods that tend to stain unevenly, such as pine or maple, lightly spray on a final mist coat and don't wipe it. Allow this coat to dry 5 minutes also.

6. Now, lift the pattern pieces from the wood as shown *below* with an X-acto knife to reveal the unstained area. Allow the project to dry overnight.

With the stain completely dry, use a clean finger to rub away any adhesive residue. If the amount of residue seems excessive, remember to make lighter applications of stain on your next project. Now, spray a light, even coat of lacquer on the entire surface. If you like the appearance of the project at this point, skip the next step and apply one more coat of lacquer to finish the piece. If you'd like to soften the contrast between the pattern area and the rest of the wood surface, proceed to the next step.

7. To enhance the country look of your project, spray another coat of stain over the entire surface and immediately wipe it with a clean cloth. The lacquered area will accept some stain, giving a subtle variation in tone between the pattern and

HALF-SIZED PATTERN
Each square = ½"

background. After allowing the surface to dry completely overnight, apply two more coats of lacquer to finish the project. *Above,* side-by-side are the two doors for our project; we skipped the final step with the door on the *right,* giving greater contrast between pattern and background.

WOOD-FINISHING PRODUCT LABELS

Only the company chemists formulating the products you apply to your woodworking projects know exactly how they'll perform. *WOOD*® magazine reader John Aversa found this out the hard way—on a kitchenful of newly installed solid pine paneling. Here's his story, plus some tips from industry insiders that will help you avoid finishing failures.

John Aversa, an experienced Palisades Park, New Jersey, woodworker, was so mad he saw red—well, bright pink anyway. He had spent many, many hours installing solid pine paneling in his kitchen, and had painstakingly worked out a blend of stains that produced the desired gray. Then, he stained the wood, waited a few days, and one evening brushed on a lacquer topcoat. It looked great. The next night, he applied more lacquer.

Daybreak brought surprise—and dismay. John's new paneling had turned a monstrous pink, with some vivid orange streaks! Following the advice of a paint store salesperson, John had mixed two different stain colors from one company and applied lacquer made by another manufacturer. Understandably upset, he complained to both manufacturers that their product labels hadn't warned him about the consequences of combining their products. To avoid John's catastrophe, read on.

In finishing, you're at risk

Bruce Hammill, chief counsel for the National Paint and Coatings Association, notes that the cautions on labels address health and fire hazards, as required by federal, state, and city laws. You'll also find content weight and measure information listed on labels. *No* regulations, however, require label information about product performance. Therefore, manufacturers feel that when a consumer uses different brands of finishing products together, as did John Aversa, they are absolved from *any* responsibility when the combination fails.

"If manufacturers covered all the ramifications of how not to use a finishing product, they'd have a label large enough to cover a 55-gallon drum on every half-pint," says Kevin Ostby of Davis Paint Co. in North Kansas City, Missouri. "Basically, a label should describe how to use a product as it comes off the shelf, such as what to do if the pigment settles."

Where to turn for the right information

With so many finishing products on the market, all with so little practical information on their labels, how do you know which ones will be best for your job?

As a rule, clerks in private-brand paint stores know their products better than those in discount stores and home centers, mainly because the employee turnover is so great in the latter," comments Joe Wolf of The Sherwin-Williams Company. "Watch the mode of response when

you ask for help," Joe advises. "If a clerk responds right way and recommends some products, he or she probably knows the right products and techniques. Conversely, if the salesperson hesitates and reaches for a can, that person probably doesn't know more than you do."

Jonathan Kemp, of H. Behlen & Bros., Inc., advises craftsmen to research: "Woodworkers read all the books and manuals on how to build the project and the best wood to buy. But, when it comes time to finish, they don't read."

Other reliable sources include local professional furniture refinishers and other woodworkers whose work has impressed you. You also can go directly to the manufacturer. Some companies maintain "hot lines" and toll-free telephone numbers to answer consumer questions. If you don't find a number listed on a label or product brochure, get it from the dealer, through the Yellow Pages, or from long-distance information. Then, call the company, ask for customer relations, and state your problem or what you want to do.

Beware the dangers of mix-and-match

The label on Brand A stain recommends following it with Brand A varnish. Does the manufacturer just want you to buy its products? "Sure, that's part of it," explains John Moser of Wood Finishing Supply Company, "but each manufacturer has its own formulation for certain products. For instance," he points out, "there can be different proportions of hot solvents, such as toluene, that have a real low flash [evaporation] point and high volatility. Therefore, his lacquer may react quite differently from another brand under certain conditions."

Bruce Jackson, a wood-finishing specialist teaching at Pittsburg State University in Kansas, elaborates, "A product may contain from three to seven different solvents. To work properly, they must flash off in a progression. If they all flash too soon, the finish could look flaky; not fast enough, the material might trap solvents."

"Stick with the same product line," stresses Behlen's Kemp. "That should ensure that Step 1 and Step 2 will work together. If they don't, there's only *one* manufacturer to deal with."

Incidentally, after a six-month delay, John Aversa completed his kitchen project. The stain manufacturer suggested he resand the wood—and offered a can of stain. The lacquer manufacturer was, from John's point of view, more understanding. They sent him $400 to cover half of all the materials involved.

In light of his experience, John advises, "Double-check everything. And, definitely don't believe just anyone's recommendations."

Tips for a top-notch finish

The experts *WOOD®* magazine talked to offered some tips to assure you a top-notch finishing job. Here's what they had to say:

Wipe down the surface. After a thorough fine-sanding, wipe down new wood with a clean rag dampened in mineral spirits before sealing or staining. James Brown, of Deft, Inc., cautions, though, against using commercially prepared tack rags, especially those claiming to be new or improved. "Too often, these contain chemicals and oils that contaminate the surface," he notes.

Never assume a clean surface. Even after sanding, wood that has had a previous finish may still have wax or silicone particles embedded in the pores that can lead to problems in the new finish. Remove these contaminants by scrubbing the wood surface with a solution of one tablespoon trisodium phosphate (TSP) and one tablespoon of household ammonia per gallon of water. After scrubbing the piece, rinse it thoroughly with clean, warm water. Sponge off remaining moisture, and allow the wood to completely dry before a final sanding. Then, just before finishing, thoroughly wipe the wood with a soft cloth dampened with mineral spirits.

Test the finish. Take a scrap of the wood you're going to finish and go through the steps, A to Z. Do the same with multicoat finishing systems because the first coat may look fine, but problems could show up in following coats.

Don't shake finishes. Shaking can create tiny bubbles that often can't be brushed out. Instead, gently stir the contents with a lifting motion to mix agents settled to the bottom.

Stir stain every five minutes. Keeping pigments mixed gives you a more uniform wood color.

Brushing takes technique. It's best to apply varnish or polyurethane with a natural-bristle brush. But, apply the finish by brushing in only one direction. Dip the bristles halfway into the varnish and touch the ends against the side of the can to drain excess. Don't drag the bristles across the can—this creates bubbles.

Know how to quit. When staining or applying a topcoat, don't quit in the middle of a large area because the eye will detect a change in color or finish. If you find a sag in a surface of varnish that has started to set up, don't rebrush. With satin-finish varnish, this causes glossy spots. Wait until it dries to apply a second coat.

Don't hurry the job. "Wait at least 24 hours" means just that. Adding a second coat too early results in a slow-drying, tacky topcoat.

LAMINATES AND VENEERS

Laminates and veneers offer you surface options that are both practical and attractive. Learn how recent innovations not only make these surfaces easier to apply, but better-looking than ever before.

CHOOSING AND BUYING PLASTIC LAMINATES

Plastic laminate has changed its face. From pinstripes to geometrics and metal look-alikes to pastels with the color solid to the core, your choices have never been more varied. To help you through the selection process, following is a rundown of what's available and what you need to know about this versatile material.

Pick the look you like

Despite tough-guy characteristics, plastic laminates have often trailed other materials as the choice when it came to up-to-date looks. But wait just a minute. Something new has been added to the mix.

Solid-to-the-core surfacing materials: Solid-core surfacing materials eliminate the unsightly, dark seam lines you have with standard laminates. Scratches and dents show up less, too, because the dings cut into a backing of the same color. With these solids, you can build up layers of varying colors for some spectacular design effects.

Metal laminates: Anodized or epoxy-coated aluminum and urethane-coated copper take on the look of bronze, gold, brass, steel, and other metals. Finishing touches can produce a look as slick as a mirror or as soft as a textured brush effect. With embossing, the metals offer a variety of designs.

Better mimics: Woodworkers will be pleased that the plastics that have masqueraded as wood look more like the real thing, thanks to improvements in printing techniques. Other look-alikes—linens, leathers, canes, slate, marble, and stone—look good, too.

Designer patterns and textures: Thus far, you won't find a Calvin Klein laminate. You may believe that designer names can't be far away, though, with the current array of patterns and textures—pinstripes, geometric patterns, graphs, embossed surfaces, and patterns that give a three-dimensional quality.

What grade laminate do you need?

• **Horizontal general-purpose laminates** stand up to the most pressure, impact, and wear with a thickness of roughly $\frac{1}{16}$". As the name implies, these laminates make the best choice for flat surfaces such as countertops or furniture tops.

• **Vertical general-purpose laminates** are thinner, less-costly surfacing materials at roughly $\frac{1}{32}$" thick. They won't take the abuse of their thicker counterpart, but they work well on walls, cabinet doors, and other similar applications. Often, you can save some money by using both horizontal- and vertical-grade sheets on a project.

• **Banding, or edge strips,** give your project an edge and save you the trouble of cutting strips. Banding comes in varying widths, but one common size measures $1\frac{7}{8}$"×12' long. Some banding is sold in foot-long strips; others, in long rolls.

• **Backing sheets** add dimensional stability to panels that aren't supported by another assembly such as a base. Ideally, the decorative plastic laminate and backing sheet should be as close in thickness as possible. The thicker the backing sheet, the greater the dimensional stability and resistance to cracking. In practice, most people cover the backs or bottoms of panels with "backing sheet," a thin, inexpensive laminate without a decorative face.

• **Cabinet liners** are less expensive than general-purpose laminates and work well inside cabinets and other casework. The liners come in limited stock colors.

• **Specialty laminates** include laminates that are fire-retardant, impervious to certain chemicals, have antistatic properties, or take more wear.

Making the purchase

Retail outlets such as home centers and lumberyards handle only a few standard sizes and designs. But they all have samples of the various patterns, so you can order from these. The largest manufacturers have distribution centers in most states, so the shipping distance may not be far. Delivery can be as short as a day or two, though some lines may take from 10 days to two weeks. In a large city, you may be able to buy directly from the manufacturer's distribution center.

Pricing: Plastic laminates are sold by the square foot. Standard patterns and wood grains typically cost between $1 and $2 a square foot. Specialty items, such as metal or solid-core colors, may cost from just under $5 to almost $7 a square foot. Price may vary according to finish. A basic matte or satin finish generally is the least expensive; higher gloss or raised finishes may cost slightly more. And, in general, backing sheets and cabinet liners cost about half what standard patterns go for.

Sizes: Standard nominal widths include 18", 24", 30", 36", 48", and 60". Standard nominal lengths are 48", 60", 72", 96", 120", and 144". Manufacturers cut sheets slightly wider and longer than stated to allow for trimming or for cutting more than one piece from a sheet. Not all products come in all widths and lengths. More specialized products may be sold in only one size sheet.

APPLYING PLASTIC LAMINATES

Do "self-respecting wood-workers" use plastic laminates? You bet they do! It's never going to replace wood as the material of choice among woodworkers, but we think you'll find it an interesting surfacing option for certain projects. And, boy, is it fun to work with!

We've divided this article into two parts. "The Basics" will serve as a refresher for those of you who have some experience with plastic laminates already (and as an introduction for those who don't). In "Nifty Solutions for Special Situations" we deal with some situations and some new materials you may not have encountered yet.

The Basics

Two ways to cut laminate down to size

1. The score-and-snap method of cutting laminate works well with all standard laminates, but not with solid-core surfacing materials. Start by laying the laminate faceup on a clean surface. Then, mark the cutoff lines, allowing at least ½ " in both directions for overhang. Put a piece of thin scrap beneath the cutoff line, locate the straightedge so that it protects the panel you'll be using, then score along a straightedge several times with a sharp-pointed tool. We use an inexpensive carbide-tipped scoring tool we bought at a local floor-covering tool supplier. When you see the dark backing showing through the color layer the entire length of the cutoff line, you're there.

2. With your hands positioned as shown and with the laminate faceup, lift up on one end of the laminate, exerting pressure until the material snaps. The photo at *center far right* shows what

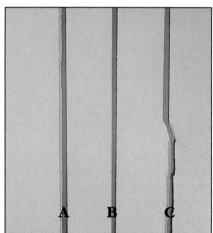

happens at the score line (a) if you press down on the laminate rather than lift up; (b) if you do as we suggest; and (c) if you don't score the laminate completely.

3. In situations where you need to cut the laminate in two or more directions, lay out and mark the cutoff lines, then drill a small hole in the scrap portion where the cutoff lines intersect. Doing this prevents you from accidentally scoring too far and also lessens the chance of stress cracks developing at the corner. Score

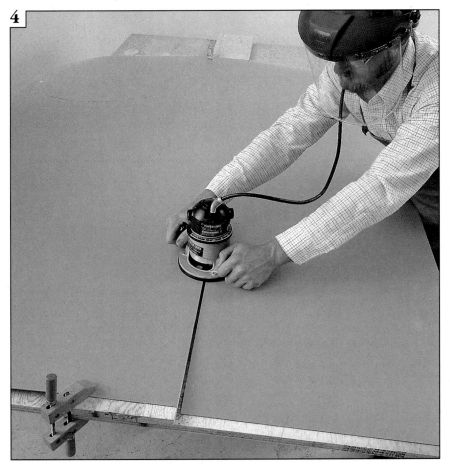

4

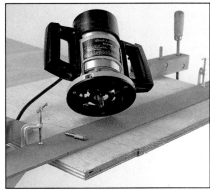

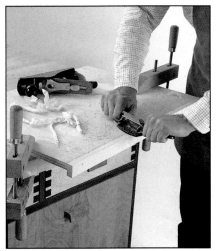

completely through the shortest dimension, then score and snap along the other.

4. We've also had good luck cutting laminate with a router fitted with a flush trimming bit. Just mark your cutoff line, clamp a straight-edge beneath the laminate, and run the router along the straightedge. You'll get a super-smooth cut.

Preparing the surface for plastic laminate

We've used both good-quality plywood and particleboard as a substrate for laminate. Regardless of which material you use, though, fill surface voids before applying the laminate. Also true up the edges and fill voids with wood putty.

The photo *above, top right* shows the setup we use to guarantee a smooth edge. This technique comes in handy if you plan to band the edges of a panel with wood.

When putting an edge banding on a shelf or countertop (see the photo, *above right)*, glue and nail

the wood to the substrate, making sure the top edge of the banding is slightly higher than the substrate. Go back later and either plane or scrape the surfaces flush. Don't use a belt sander; it may gouge the surface or round over an edge.

Applying the adhesive and laminate

1. Because you want to minimize the visual impact of the joint lines, the sequence of application is every bit as important as the technique. As a general rule, cover the under-side of a panel first, the back and side edges, the front edge, and finish with the top surface. Contact cement sets up quickly, so on all but very small projects we recom-mend using a narrow, short-napped roller as shown in photo A on *page 86*. Give both mating surfaces one liberal coat of contact cement (use only the nonflammable type), then allow the adhesive to dry. How do you know when the surfaces are ready for contact? Give them the

touch test! If the adhesive sticks to your finger when you touch it, it's not ready.

2. To keep from mispositioning the laminate on the substrate, we lay venetian blind slats between the substrate and the laminate (see photo B). Once we have laid the laminate into position and have checked to make sure we have excess to trim off on all edges, we withdraw the slats one at a time. Smooth the laminate with one hand as you work toward the other end.

3. If for some reason you goof, we've found that you can retrieve laminate even if it's already made contact (see photo C). With a spray bottle partially full of contact spray, dust a fine mist of solvent along the edge. Then, lift up the edge with a putty knife. Continue spraying and lifting, and the substrate and laminate will part company. Allow the solvent to evaporate, recoat both the laminate and substrate, and re-lay the laminate.

continued

APPLYING PLASTIC LAMINATES
continued

4. After the substrate and laminate make contact, you want to ensure a good bond between the two. Though you can accomplish this by tapping the entire surface with a scrap block and hammer, we use a rubber J-roller. With it, we can apply a lot of pressure, and we also avoid the problem of fracturing the laminate at the edges (photo D), which is a possibility with the other method.

Trimming and finishing off the edges

We've trimmed laminate with carbide-tipped flush-trimming router bits with ball-bearing pilots, but we can honestly say that a much less expensive solid carbide bit with a solid pilot works just as well for us. And that's the opinion of some professionals we've talked to as well. With either type bit, you've got to be on guard against burning or scratching adjoining surfaces. We've found the two best strategies here are to keep the router moving and to apply a layer of petroleum jelly to the surface that the bearing guides against before routing off the excess. Theoretically, a router bit with a ball bearing guide should prevent mishaps. But as you trim an edge, for example, the contact cement builds up and restricts the movement of the bearing.

Trimming laminates with a flush trimming bit results in a sharp, square edge. For safety's sake, dress the edge with a single-cut file as shown *opposite, bottom.* Hold the file so that the edge will be beveled slightly, and move the file across the edge lightly several times.

A

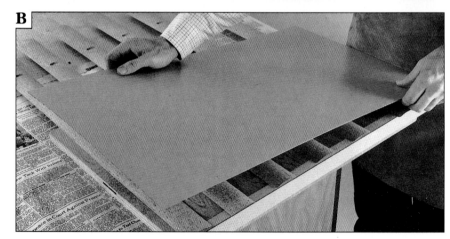

B

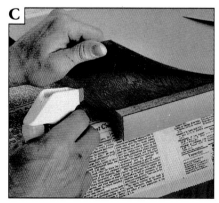

C

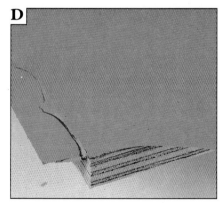

D

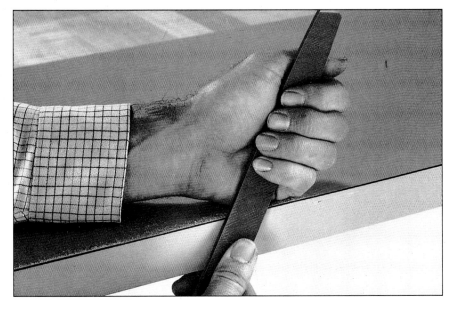

More tips on working with laminates

• Before working with plastic laminate or the newer solid-color surfacing materials, allow a day or so for the material to acclimate. Also make sure that the contact cement is at room temperature before applying it.

• Be *extra* careful when handling and working the solid-color surfacing materials. They're even more brittle than standard laminates. They also have the habit of chipping when being cut, so use sharp, carbide-tipped cutters when cutting or shaping them. And if you glue several layers of these materials together to create decorative edge treatments, be sure to scuff up the face of the layers to which other material will be applied to ensure a good bond.

• If you apply laminate to any surface that won't be anchored securely to another assembly, always apply laminate, or the less-expensive "backing sheet," to the back side of the panel to minimize the chances of warping due to moisture.

• Always work in a well-ventilated area when applying contact cement, as its vapors can be dizzying if inhaled for too long a period. And don't work around heat or flames.

• Sometimes air bubbles form between the laminate and the substrate after application and cause the bond to break. (Usually the cause of this is laying down the laminate before the cement has "flashed off.") To correct this situation, lay a damp cloth over the area in question, then place an iron set at the cotton setting onto the cloth. Doing this reactivates the cement and allows you to press the laminate and substrate together.

• To help prevent stress cracks at inside corners, hold the contact cement back about 6" in all directions from the corner, then apply white glue to both surfaces and clamp them together.

• To keep the contact cement applicator relatively pliable between coats, wrap it in plastic to keep the solvent from escaping.

Nifty Solutions for Special Situations

Wrapping laminate around corners

Ever wonder if you could wrap plastic laminate around a relatively tight radius? We were curious to find out, so one of the staffers brought in a blow dryer to see if we could do a little coaxing by heating the laminate. Nothing doing; it didn't heat the laminate to the 313-degree temperature that postforming manuals specify as the correct laminate bending

continued

APPLYING PLASTIC LAMINATES
continued

temperature. So we got hold of a commercial heat gun at a local rental outlet. With it, we formed the laminate around radii down to about 1". We bent the laminate first, then applied contact cement.

Wrapping a cylinder

Start by cutting the laminate to the length and width required. Be sure to allow extra for trimming. Apply contact cement to both mating surfaces, wait until the cement is dry to the touch, and apply the laminate to the substrate, except for the last 8 to 10". Slip a piece of waxed paper beneath the laminate, then carefully mark both edges of the laminate as shown.

Carefully align one edge of a straightedge with the marks you just made, and clamp the straightedge in place as shown. Run your router along the edge.

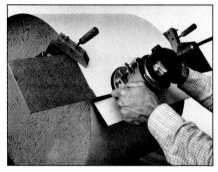

Picture-perfect joint lines

When you want a perfect joint line between two pieces of laminate that butt end-to-end or edge-to-edge, try this technique: Clamp two pieces of scrap to your workbench with a small space between them, then butt the two pieces of laminate together. Now secure the pieces of laminate with two more scrap lumber cleats. One pass with your router fitted with a carbide trimming bit, and you've got it made. Hold the router against one of the guides, and don't rotate the base of the router because many bases are not perfectly round.

Aligning geometric-patterned laminates

One of the new-generation "designer" laminates, the geometrics can cause you headaches if you're not careful. To make them look good, the surfaces you adhere them to must be square. This, combined with the fact that the patterns themselves aren't always true, makes aligning these laminates difficult. To make things easier on ourselves, we cut four like-sized wood scraps, and use them as shown. We make any needed adjustments, then apply contact cement to both of the surfaces and then lower the laminate down onto the substrate.

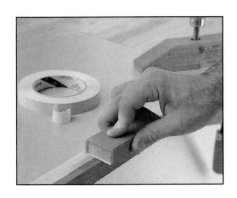

Hiding unsightly seam lines and defects

What if you end up with a less-than-perfect joint line or need to repair a defect of some sort? We decided to try a product called Kampel SEAMFIL from a local laminate retailer. We color-mixed some according to the directions and forced it into a seam. It worked as advertised, although we did have quite a time getting a color match. If we used the product again, we'd pay to have the factory color-match the product for us to guarantee good results.

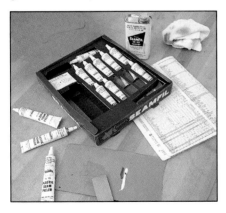

Finish-sanding wooden edge banding

When you choose the option of dressing up the edge of a shelf or counter with a wood banding, getting the wood perfectly flush with the top of the laminate is tricky. When we apply the banding, we try to make sure the wood

projects a bit above the laminate. Then we mask off the laminate and use a sanding block to bring the two surfaces flush. When we begin to see scuff marks on the masking tape, we call it quits.

Dressing up the edges of textured laminates

You can trim the edges of textured laminates as you do other laminates, but the bearing or pilot will follow all of the depressions and other irregularites in the material along the way. We dress the edge by working a triangular file carefully as shown here. A time-consuming technique to be sure, but necessary when working with these kinds of textured patterns.

Three common countertop problems

Countertop installations give most people fits, mainly because the walls countertops fit up against are irregular. But scribing to fit allows you to compensate for those imperfections. In the instance shown *top right,* we used a thin piece of scrap material and a pencil to scribe the irregularities of both walls onto the laminate.

Most laminate-trimming routers can't trim laminate right up to the wall. To trim the remainder of the excess material, we guide our scoring tool along a straightedge several times until we work our way through the material. Then we put the finishing touches on with a file.

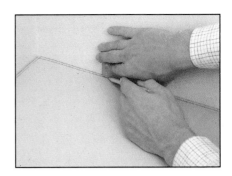

Here's a tip for when you install a sink in a countertop. We mark the cutoff lines, then bore a ½" hole in each corner of the cutout. These holes do two things. First, they provide a radius at each inside corner, which helps to prevent stress cracking. And they also prevent you from accidentally scoring surrounding laminate. We score along each of the cutoff lines, then use a jigsaw with a metal-cutting blade to cut out the top. (This blade reduces chip-out.)

WORKING WITH FLEXIBLE WOOD VENEERS

Goodbye, veneer presses, long glue-drying times, and random-width strips that require straight-line ripping before application. Hello, paper-thin backed real wood veneer.

You can apply this factory-matched and machined product over existing furniture pieces, cabinets, and other such items to make them look brand-new. Or, on new projects, lay it down over an inexpensive substrate when you want the look of a beautiful domestic or imported wood—easily and more quickly than you might have thought possible.

We think that inexperienced and veteran woodworkers alike will appreciate the many merits of this thin-skinned, flexible material. And as you'll realize after you read through this article, learning to apply it correctly and expertly doesn't take long at all. You should have good success the very first time you use it.

The tools and materials you'll need

One of the things we like so much about backed flexible wood veneers is that we don't have to have lots of expensive equipment to get the job done. The photo *below* shows what you'll need. You can buy other specialized tools, if you want, but you can achieve good results with what you see here.

You won't need many tools

Because flexible veneer measures a minute ⅟₁₆" thick, you can cut it easily with a sharp-bladed crafts knife. We make many of our cuts using a cork-backed steel ruler (the cork keeps the ruler from sliding around on the veneer). The masking tape keeps mating pieces of veneer stabilized while cutting and while butting together the edges of two adjoining pieces.

You'll need some solvent-base contact cement (the nonflammable type), a supply of waxed paper, and an inexpensive brush or roller for applying the cement (we like a roller best for large projects). And to make sure that the veneer bonds well to the substrate, you'll need a scrap wood tap block and a mallet and/or a commercially available veneer roller.

And finally, just in case you position the veneer incorrectly when you lay it down (accidents do happen occasionally), you'll want to have a syringe and needle and some refinisher handy to help lift off the veneer. Both of these products contain a chemical that breaks the bond of the contact cement quickly and easily.

Preparing the surface for the veneer

No matter what material you put veneer onto—solid wood, plywood, particleboard, or hardboard—the surface must be smooth. If it's not,

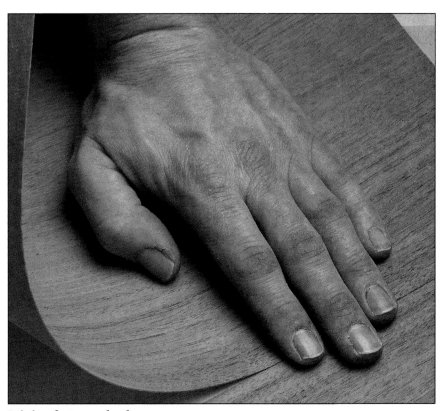

Joining factory-edged veneer

chances are good that those bumps and bruises will telegraph through the veneer.

If you're putting a new face on an old furniture piece or cabinet front, start by filling in any indentations in the surface and regluing any splintered wood or loose veneer. We've had good luck with hard putty for filling holes and other blemishes. (If the piece is in terrible shape, you may be best off removing loose veneer.) Then, sand the surface smooth, and remove the resulting sawdust with a few blasts of air from an air compressor hose or with a tack cloth. With projects under construction, the procedures remain essentially the same.

Note: If you plan to shape the edges of a project in which you've used one of the composition materials (or a solid wood other than the veneer species) as a substrate, you'll want to add an edging to those surfaces that will be shaped. (We use a solid wood edging of the same species as the veneer.) Be sure to figure in the width of the edging when determining the size of the various substrate parts.

Making up for width

Though you can mail-order flexible veneer in sheets up to 4'✕12', you'll find yourself in situations from time to time in which you'll need to edge-join two narrow pieces of veneer.

Joining manufactured edges

From the factory, flexible veneers come with straight edges that make joining two pieces quite manageable. Of course, before doing anything, you should check to make sure that they haven't been banged up in any way.

Start by butting the two pieces together and settling on a grain match that appeals to you. Then, turn over one of the mating pieces and lay down a piece of masking tape so that about half of it overlaps the seam line. Now, turn that same piece over and butt the edge of the mating piece up against it as shown in the photo *above*. To make sure you have a good bond between the tape and the veneer, run your fingernail along the seam *continued*

WORKING WITH FLEXIBLE WOOD VENEERS
continued

Overlapping veneer with irregular edges

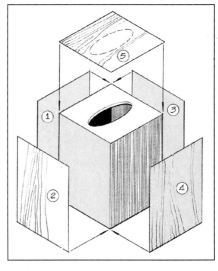

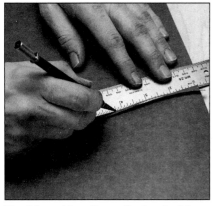

Double-cutting from the back side

line. (If you don't like the way the joint turned out, just pull the pieces apart and have at it again.)

If everything looks good, lay a strip of masking tape along the front side of the joint line (this stays put until you apply the veneer), and remove the tape from the back side. That's all there is to it; you're ready to apply the veneer as a single piece.

Joining pieces with irregular edges

Especially when you're working with small, leftover pieces of veneer, you won't usually have straight edges to work with. But

with flexible veneers, that's not a handicap in the least. Simply lay out the mating pieces, face up, and overlap them by ½" or so (make sure that you're satisfied with the grain match).

Now, tape the two pieces together with masking tape as shown in the photo *above.* Turn the veneer over, then once you're certain you know where the two pieces overlap, cut through both thicknesses of veneer with a sharp-bladed crafts knife, as shown *at left.* (You can do this freehand, if you want; actually, it's harder for the eye to see a crooked line than a straight one.)

Carefully remove the scrap pieces and fit the mating pieces together to check for a good fit. When you're satisfied, join the pieces with masking tape.

Applying the veneer

Note: *When veneering a tabletop, cabinet door, shelf, or any other "floating" element, you must veneer both sides to keep it in balance. Veneering only one side may result in warping. You can save money by using a less-expensive veneer on the back side or underside.*

Before you actually apply contact cement to the veneer or the substrate, you must first determine the sequence of application. Let's take a simple example to illustrate. Say you want to veneer a tissue box cover like the one shown *above.* You would start by veneering the back, then move to the sides, then the front, and finally the top. By progressing in this order, you minimize the effect of the seams.

And to minimize waste, lay the veneer facedown on a flat surface, and lay the object to be veneered on top of the veneer. Trace the outline of the object as shown *below,* then cut the veneer a bit over-size (we allow at least ½" all around).

Apply two coats of contact cement to the veneer and the substrate, allowing time to dry between coats. (Some brands of contact cement lose their gloss when they dry; others dry clear.)

Now (especially if you're veneering a surface of any size), gently lay a sheet of kraft paper, waxed paper, or freezer paper onto the substrate as shown *below*. (Doing this prevents the veneer from grabbing the substrate before you want it to.) Remember, it's difficult to separate them.

Note: *For obvious reasons, we recommend that you use a nonflammable contact cement and that you work in a well-ventilated area. We've had quite good luck with 3M's Fast Bond 30, a nonflammable, nonodorous product, as well as Constantine's Veneer Glue.*

Carefully align the veneer over the substrate, then press the veneer into place. Withdraw the paper an inch or two at a time and continue pressing the veneer from side to side as shown at *left bottom* until the entire surface has been covered. Continue to smooth the veneer with your hands, checking for any trapped air bubbles while doing so. If you spot any of them, slit the veneer along the grain with your crafts knife as shown in the photo *below left*. Then, press toward the slit with your fingers to remove the trapped air.

To make sure that there's a good bond between the substrate and the veneer, tap the surface with a block and mallet as shown *below,* or roll it with a commercially available veneer roller. (Work from one end to the other, or from the center out, again watching for bubbles).

Easing veneer into place

Deflating air bubbles

Ensuring good contact.

Now, trim the excess veneer that overhangs the edges. We usually lay the veneered surface facedown on a backing block and trim the excess. But you can also cut the excess away as shown in the photo on *page 94, top left*. (Some *WOOD*® staffers prefer a veneer saw to do the trimming; others like a crafts knife because they insist it does as good a job, and does it much more quickly We haven't had any problems with the knife veering off and following the grain.)

Once you have finished trimming the veneer, sand it with a sanding block fitted with 80-grit sandpaper. Make sure you don't round-over the edges as you're sanding. And don't sand too long in any one spot. Remember, you're dealing with a 1/64"-thick layer of wood.

continued

Pressing the veneer from side to side

WORKING WITH FLEXIBLE WOOD VENEERS
continued

Trimming panel edge

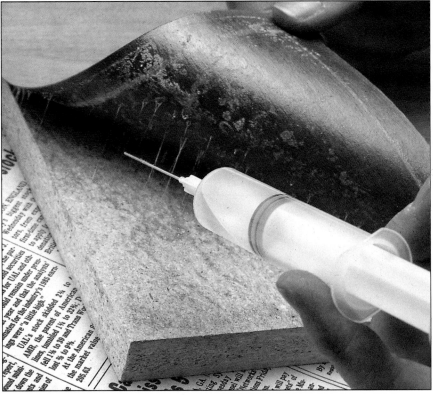

Using refinisher to release the bond.

What to do if things go wrong during application

Nothing is perfect, right! It could happen that when applying the veneer, you misjudge its position, and before you realize it, the contact cement on both surfaces has made contact. Don't panic!

If you realize you've made a mistake before the veneer is completely down, lay hold of your refinisher-filled syringe. Spread some of the refinisher along the point of contact as shown in the photo *above right*, then carefully lift off the veneer.

Sometimes you won't notice that the veneer didn't cover the substrate entirely until it is completely down. In this case, you simply patch the uncovered area with a scrap piece of veneer as shown at *right*. Of course, you'll want to be sure to carefully match the grain before butting the patch piece against the other veneer.

Applying solid wood edgings

Start by cutting the material the same thickness as the material you're attaching it to, and just a bit wider than necessary to accommodate the shaped edge. Then, glue and clamp the edging material, but only after making sure its thickness matches the mating material. After the glue has dried, sand all surfaces flush and smooth.

Patching a mistake.

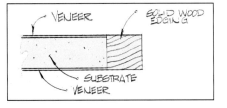

How to finish your veneered project

As with any other woodworking project, the smoother the surface when you apply the finish, the better the finished product will look. Fortunately, flexible veneers are sanded smooth at the factory, so a light finish-sanding will do. If you have routed the edges of the work, careful hand-sanding is in order.

You can stain, fill, and finish flexible veneers, but keep in mind that oil and contact cement don't get along too well. If oil penetrates the veneer and makes contact with the adhesive, you can be certain delamination will occur. We've found that several thin coats of polyurethane varnish make a good topcoat for veneered projects. (Some veneer experts insist that you can apply oil finishes sparingly with good results, but we haven't had much luck with oil-base products.)

Note: As always, test the finishing products on scrap to see what finish they will produce before applying them to your project.

HOW TO MAKE A FLUSH PATCH ON OLD VENEER

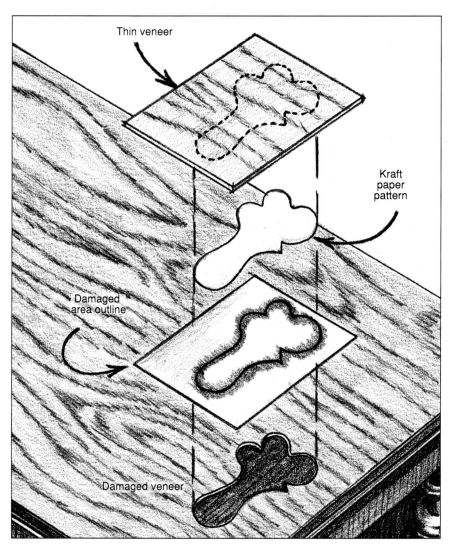

Thin veneer

Kraft paper pattern

Damaged area outline

Damaged veneer

O ld and antique furniture was made with thicker veneer than you'll find today. That causes a problem if you try to make a patch during a refinishing or restoration project. Don't worry, though! We've found a solution that should make your repair job a real success.

With help from high-tech machinery, today's veneer manufacturers make the most out of ever-more-expensive veneer logs by slicing them onion-skin thin. That's great for them! But when you repair a "veteran" veneered surface—typically $\frac{1}{16}$" thick—you somehow have to bridge the thickness gap between it and the new, thinner material.

At *WOOD®*, we use a backing of heavy-duty kraft paper (grocery sacks work fine). Glued to the back of thin veneer, it forms a tough support for an otherwise fragile patch. Usually, you'll have to shim up the $\frac{1}{128}$"-thick material in order for the patch to match at the proper level.

Follow these steps for a real pro repair:

1. Clean out the damaged area by cutting away the old veneer with a sharp craft, utility, or trimming knife. Make an irregular outline for the patch area if you can. It'll be less noticeable than a circular or rectangular area when you're finished. Be sure to scrape away any old glue and splinters left from the veteran veneer.

2. Cut a piece of kraft paper larger than you need for the patch. Place this paper over the patch area, hold it firmly in place, and rub around the patch outline with a soft lead pencil. To form a pattern for the patch, trim the paper carefully along the pencil line. Now test fit it.

3. Select a piece of new veneer that matches as closely as possible the grain and coloring of the original veneer. Next, adhere your kraft paper pattern to the back of the new veneer with contact cement. Watch out so you don't flop the pattern in the process— the *top* of the pattern gets attached to the *back* of the veneer! Also remember to arrange the veneer on the pattern so the grain direction matches that of the original surface.

4. Trim the veneer to match your pattern outline, then fit it into the damaged area. You may have to do some additional trimming for an exact fit.

5. Dry-fit the patch to see if it sits slightly above the surface to allow for some sanding. If it doesn't, add more layers of kraft paper to shim it up.

6. Glue the patch in with contact cement, firmly rolling or pressing it down. When it's dry, you can sand and complete the finishing of the patched area.

ACKNOWLEDGMENTS

Writers

John Arno—Finishing Pine for an Early American Look, page 71

Jim Barrett—Get Smooth Results from your Belt Sander, page 9

George Brandsberg—Modern-Day Crackling, page 61; Wood Finishing Product Labels, pages 80–81

James Hufnagel—Off with the Old, pages 5–8

Larry Johnston—A Carver's Guide to Acrylics, pages 74–75

Bill Krier—Time Tested Strategies for Removing Wood Finishes, pages 10–11; Getting Under the Surface of Today's Finish Removers, pages 12–15; Painted Stone Finishes, pages 62–64

Bill Krier with Jim Downing— Sanding Shortcuts, pages 20–25, Five Easy Steps to a Finish That's Glass Smooth, pages 38–39

Bill Krier with Wade Sundeen, Jim Downing and Jim Boelling—Water-Based Finishes, pages 55–59

Bill Krier with Dick Fitch and Jim Boelling—Country Finishes, pages 66–70

Peter J. Stephano—Analine Dyes, pages 76–77

Gary A. Zeff—In Search of the Perfect Finish, pages 31–32

Photographers

Bill Kern Photography
Bob Calmer
Richard Faverty
Tom Gann
Reddie Henderson
John Hetherington
Hopkins Associates
Jim Kascoutas
Plasti-Kote, Inc.
Bob Stites
Perry Struse
Gary A. Zeff

Illustrators

Advertising Art Studios Inc.
Herb Dixon
Jim Downing
Kim Downing
C. L. Gatzke
Mike Henry
Jim Stevenson

If you would like to order any additional copies of our books, call 1-800-678-2802 or check with your local bookstore.
